"<u>Through The Eyes of Santa</u>, Robert C. ences as Santa's helper, is absolutely d accumulated over thirty years of loving to the next one! I became so caught up in his accounts of the children, aided by Goodman's warm and friendly style of writing, that I found myself weeping with heartbreak one moment and laughing with joy the next. What wonderful things he—and the children—have done. What a tribute he gives to all those men and women who so generously put on the red suit at Christmas time! This is a must-read for everyone, particularly those who may have lost that sweetly innocent belief in dear old Santa and the miracles he helps bring to pass!"

—Blaine M. Yorgason, author of *The Windwalker, Charlie's Monument* and *One Tattered Angel*

"In my 24 years of active duty I've had a variety of assignments with some fantastic individuals. What really stands out is one of the most blessed days in my life when I served as RC Goodman's Christmas elf. From my 6' 5" very bright green vantage point, I witnessed the pure joy Santa brought to hundreds of children, including my own two little girls. Seeing children smile and hearing them laugh and truly believe in RC's Santa has no price tag. Just like the stories in this book, RC... you are priceless!"

—Richard "Dicko" Stevens, Colonel, USAF Retired; F-16 Test Pilot, Edwards AFB, California

"Santa has a sharp eye for storytelling in this account of Goodman's moving experiences with children as they struggle with illness and abuse, as well as questions of belief and, ultimately, joy. From Vietnam to the Mojave Desert of California, his short, concise accounts of impossible wishes made real and funny answers to skeptical children are timeless."

—William F. Wu, Ph.D., author of the series, *Isaac Asimov's Robots in Time*

There's a reason his last name is GOOD MAN. RC continues to bring good life to this old world. These stories only scratch the surface of the lives this Santa's helper in the red suit has touched. God bless you RC and for heaven sakes, quit peeing in the bushes!!!"

—Francis "Fuzzy" Zeller, Major, USAF Retired; F-16 Fighter Pilot

"RC Goodman is a natural born storyteller. He is also a natural Santa Claus, in the flesh. Readers of all faiths will be inspired and maybe get a little misty at these true tales of authentic Christmas spirit."

—Dennis Anderson, author of the novels *Target Stealth, Blackbird* and *Arthur King*; Journalist of Year Special Honor 2004, Suburban Newspapers of America

"Mr. Goodman, AKA Santa, deserves a humanitarian medal for his outstanding contribution of bringing Christmas cheer to thousands of kids throughout America. The stories in this book are so unique and heartwarming, I could not put it down until I finished it."

—Ronald K. Mortimer, Aviation Machinist Mate, Senior Chief, USNR

"I had no idea that being a Santa's helper was so involving. After reading this book, I have great respect for anyone who participates as a helper during the Christmas holidays. It's destined to become a classic that adults and children alike can enjoy for years to come."
　　—Richard Traugh, Proprietor, Protech Auto Service, Tehachapi, California

"I've known RC for many years and have heard several of these stories. He has a heart of gold, the wit of Red Skelton and the compassion of a saint. I'm dubious whenever he calls and says, "Hey Bubba, what are you doing right now?" but truly honored to know and call him my friend."
　　—William "Bubba" Francis, helicopter pilot to the rich and famous

"Robert Goodman brings the Santa Claus legend new perspective. Did you ever wonder what it would be like to actually be Santa in the eyes of thousands of kids? Goodman lets you know, in a sincere and dedicated true story of his experiences in the red suit. You'll find it funny and sweet and very human. It's a terrific Christmas gift from Santa himself."
　　—Adam West, actor, classic Batman

"Robert Goodman is the epitome of humanity. His stories show the need that children and adults have for Santa's love and acceptance during the holidays. You will smile, cry and laugh at times, but feel better knowing that Santa gave a bit more joy to all these people."
　　—Jon C. Watson, CDR, SC, USNR

"You don't believe in Santa Claus? Then you haven't read <u>Through the Eyes of Santa</u>! In this book, RC Goodman captures the true essence of the REAL Saint Nick. I was proud to be RC's first (and largest) supersonic sleigh-driving green elf, and witnessed him bring joy and wonder to the eyes of hundreds of kids at a time. Now this book brings RC's magic to millions more!"
　　—Joe Sobczak, Lt. Colonel, USAF Retired; Flight Test Captain, United Airlines

"Children are our greatest asset, and their memories of how Santa touched their lives during times of need will be remembered. RC is no ordinary Santa. He is an angel in a red suit."
　　—Phyllis R. Porter, Support Account Management Spec., United States Postal Service, Headquarters, Washington, DC; Storekeeper First Class, USNR

"RC brings me to laughter and tears with his memories of being Santa. There are things in this book that I think my two boys said, things that I wish they had said, and things that I hope they never said (but, unfortunately, probably did). Only RC knows, since he was Santa to them. Thanks, RC, for being Santa, and thanks for telling us what you learned."
　　—Ron "Taco" Johnston, B-2 Stealth Test Pilot

Through the Eyes of Santa

Stories From a Veteran Santa's Helper

by
Robert Clifton Goodman, Jr.

Aslan
PUBLISHING

Fairfield, CT

Aslan Publishing
2490 Black Rock Turnpike, #342
Fairfield, CT 06825
Please contact the publisher for a free catalog.
Phone: **203/372-0300**
Fax: **203/374-4766**
www.aslanpublishing.com

Library of Congress Cataloging-in-Publication Data

Goodman, Robert C.
  Through the eyes of Santa : stories from a veteran Santa's helper / by
Robert Clifton Goodman.
     p. cm.
  ISBN 0-944031-96-X
  1. Santa Claus. 2. Santa Claus--Humor. 3. Santa Claus--Pictorial works.
4. Christmas stories. I. Title.

GT4985.G583 2004
394.2663--dc22

                    2004052978

Editing and book design by Dianne Schilling
Cover design by Miggs Burroughs
Printing by Baker Johnson, Inc.
Printed in the USA

In Memory of
"Bob"
Robert Clifton Goodman Sr.
March 2, 1921 — January 3, 2001

I dedicate this book to the memory of a man I appreciated and adored—my wonderful father. There will be only one Bob Goodman Sr. in the annals of history and I am proud to say he was my Dad, a mentor to all who knew him. He was not only a true Santa to me and my siblings, he was a godsend to other families on our street, always willing to give of his heart and money to see that people in need received an evening meal, especially on holidays.

We called Dad the "donut man" because he showed up daily, often after a hard day's work, with a big box of donuts for his children, friends, and needy families. You could not have found a bigger-hearted individual on the face of the earth.

He is gone now, no doubt fitted with wings of gold to fly with the other angels in Heaven. When his time on earth was over the Almighty definitely received a man of honor and one who made a difference in life.

A small tag is attached to a flower arrangement at my father's gravesite in Clinton, Tennessee. It reads: "Always Loved, Never Forgotten, And In Our Hearts Forever—Mom, Bobby, Ronnie, & Daddy's Lil' Girl, Susie."

Acknowledgments

Many people urged me to write this book. Without encouragement and support from loved ones, friends and the parents of many of the children I've served, I dare say these pages would not exist. For those who know my heart and work as a Santa's helper, thank you for being there when I needed you most.

Deepest gratitude to my family: Annie, a wonderful spouse and the love of my life; my mother, Faye; Grandma Emma; Ron; Susie; my children Robert III, Margie and Dawn Ann; and all the grandchildren.

Thanks to my close friends: Scott V. Stewart and his family; Bill (Bubba) Francis; Master Sergeant Bill Macauley IV; Ann Thompson; Tony Becktel, a gifted writer and comrade; and many others.

I shall not forget Mr. Mark Anzalone who helped make the original manuscript presentable.

My gratitude to Barbara and Hal Levine of Aslan Publishing for making this book possible, to Dianne Schilling for her superb editing and book design, and to Miggs Burroughs for the outstanding cover.

To all: I have done my best!

Author's Note

In this book I have endeavored to share with readers what it is like to wear the Santa suit each Christmas. For over thirty years, I have been a Santa's helper and the stories I can relate are boundless. The most difficult part of writing the book was deciding which stories to tell. The ones I have chosen are unique. Some are truly incredible.

This is not an autobiography. It is mostly about the look-a-like state I achieve as Santa. What's more, the greater part of each chapter is about the children, and about circumstances that in some cases seem hopeless until assistance arrives in unusual ways from a Santa's helper. I believe that these stories must be told so that future generations will know the true meaning of Christmas and the love my generation has for humanity.

This book is safe for young eyes. Keep it on any bookshelf or display it on the coffee table. I have not given away any holiday secrets, especially concerning Santa. Childhood does not last long these days, and children will learn those facts soon enough. Rest assured I have taken great care to protect the myths and legend of old Saint Nick.

This book was also written with appreciation for all the Santa's helpers across the world. For those who wear the suit at Christmas, I say from my heart—read and enjoy. If my stories remind you of your own experiences, remember that I have walked in your shoes. Like you, I know the happy times, and the heartbreak of a child's tears.

x

Contents

Introduction

What Is a Santa's Helper?

Jolly old Saint Nick, Santa Claus, Kris Kringle. Mention any of these names to a child or adult, and the listener invariably smiles. No less than a billion people around the world know who he is, where he lives and what he looks like. They even remember the names of his reindeer. Yet ask these same people who their local member of Congress is, or whether their town mayor is a Democrat or Republican, or what state the President is from and a puzzled look will cross the faces of many. Santa, the name most individuals prefer to use, has been around ages longer than any of these public officials. He is a jovial character without creed, nationality or political favor. How could anyone fail to love a gentleman like that?

Every December children and their parents visit malls, churches, schools and numerous other places that Santa frequents during the weeks prior to his famous Christmas Eve trip. Did you ever ask where all of those Santas come from? All those men (and a few women) participate in the yearly holiday ritual of their own free will to promote a happy family atmosphere at Christmas.

It is against the laws of nature for any person (even Santa) to occupy more than one earth-space at a time, so this miraculous omnipresence is accomplished with helpers. Thousands of people gladly give up their day jobs a few weeks before Christmas for the benefit of children. This gives old Santa the time he needs to memorize maps of each and every town, city and rural area around the world. It's not an easy job to ensure that all children are included on his list of stops. So in essence, Santa's identical helpers are his eyes in the field. Everything we see, the identity of each child we talk to, and all the toy orders are relayed through telepathic means directly to the North Pole. People marvel that Santa knows who has been naughty or nice. Now you understand how this spectacular feat is accomplished.

Santa's helpers do not just raise their hands and say, "I'm ready, Santa, put me to work! Let the little ones come and sit on my knee so I may hear their Christmas dreams." That is a far cry from the way helpers are chosen.

Prospective helpers are rigorously tested. How they talk, walk, perform, and behave around children is carefully scrutinized. Are their hearts pure, free from lust, greed and the influence of modern obsessions? Santa is no fool and accepts only applicants of the finest character. A big heart is necessary for this job, and a good deal of integrity, because the special gifts given to helpers by Santa must be used strictly for their intended purposes.

"There is no bending the rules," Santa tells all new helpers. "When you are with my children you are me. No foolishness or skullduggery will be tolerated. Remember, I see *all* through every helper's eyes—I feel the touch of little hands upon your suit. I smell the innocence of youth through your nostrils. You are me when wearing that red suit and I know your heart through your actions."

Why do we pay homage to a man who visits us only during the Christmas holiday? Why doesn't he visit year 'round? Because Christmas is the celebration of the birth of

Jesus. Everyone who knows the story of Jesus remembers the three wise men who came bearing gifts for the newborn child. See the resemblance? Santa makes his yearly run on Christmas Eve, the night celebrated for the birth of Jesus. Not surprisingly, like the three wise-men he is the bearer of gifts for loved ones around the world.

In a way, Santa is the wise man of today and tomorrow—a giver of love and cheer throughout the world. He subtly reminds Christians to observe the true significance of December 25.

Skeptics tell us that Santa is no more than a myth, a legend, a classic clown who dresses as though more at home in a traveling circus than a modern mall. May I remind those individuals of the 1947 movie, *Miracle on 34th Street*, which delivered a very important message largely forgotten over the years? The United States Postal Service, the largest mail delivery service in the world, receives millions of letters yearly, all addressed to Santa at his residence near the North Pole. Isn't it common sense that if Santa were a figment of our imaginations all those letters would be returned to the individual sender stamped, "address unknown"? Of course. And how many letters are actually returned? Zero is the correct answer.

Yes, Santa is real, and without his blessing this book would not have been possible. As I am one of his devoted helpers, Santa can rest assured that the first copy off the press will be sent directly to the North Pole—autographed, naturally!

Along with candy canes and gifts, Santa gives children special words of encouragement and tips for staying on the "nice" list.

Chapter One

Key to the Gates of Heaven

Part 1

Santa lookalikes seldom have the privilege of choosing when or where they will ply their knowledge, yet we do what we do with open hearts. If a hospital needs an evening visit from the bearded fellow, we perform our duty without hesitation. But when I was called to a cancer ward filled with little ones, my vision of what to expect could not have been further from the truth.

Cancer is a dreaded illness that chooses its victims randomly—rich and poor, young and old, male and female, black, brown and white. No one can hide from this menace. This was my first visit to such a ward, and I learned a lesson that humbles me to this day.

Entertaining a child whose life is ending, whether by accident, disease, or divine intervention, is the toughest road a Santa's helper walks. I say with conviction, and I believe I speak for all Santa's helpers across the world, all children have the same gifts of faith and imagination no matter what their individual circumstances. The unfortunate ones, I admit, get a little extra attention and love.

I was standing in the hallway a few feet from a patient's room, dressed in my Santa attire. I fought to keep from turning around and heading back out to the parking lot. I told myself that leaving would be cowardly, something a snake in the grass would do, and purposely pushed the rotten idea out of my head. Scared half to death about seeing a dying child, the only thing I could do was be myself, laugh, smile and try to bring happiness. I knew that this child would probably never see Santa again.

Straightening my coat, the goodie-bag slung over my shoulder, I took a deep breath and knocked hard three times on the partially open door. "Ho, ho, ho," I bellowed. "Merry Christmas to everyone."

The shriek of a woman followed by a plastic bedpan hitting the wall stopped my heart in mid-beat.

"Get out of here you pervert," the elderly woman screamed from her bed. She turned her back to me, her split hospital gown exposing a wrinkled sight that gave new meaning to the phrase, half moon rising. I flushed with embarrassment. No cheek-rouge needed this evening. Obviously I was in the wrong room.

"You're in the right hospital, Santa," laughed a female voice behind me. "I believe the room you want is next door." She sounded like a low-toned hyena with a hiccup.

I turned to face a large-boned nurse who resembled more a tackle for the Chicago Bears than a loving caregiver of little people. "I, uh, got the wrong room."

"That's what I figured," she said. "You're early aren't you?"

"Yes, yes I am. I thought it best to get an early start. I've never done a gig like this, so I don't know how much time I'll need with the kids."

"Gig," a puzzled look crossed her face. "What's a gig?"

"A job," I said, hurriedly closing the door. "I call all my Santa jobs gigs."

She mustered a corner-of-the-mouth smile, her expression telling me she still did not understand. "Whatever, Santa. Follow me and I'll introduce you to Braids. By the way, I'm Candy. I spoke to you on the phone about doing this... gig."

I tightened my grip on the goodie-bag. "Nice to put a face with a voice. Braids? Is that this little one's real name?" We moved to the next partly open doorway.

"That's right, Santa. By the way, I suggest you refrain from mentioning anything about her loss of hair," Candy sighed. "Poor thing. Chemo really got hold of her this time. You know she's..."

"Yes, you mentioned over the phone that one of the kids would be leaving us soon."

Nurse Candy gave me a hard stare. "We gave her a private room, Santa. Do what you can to cheer her up. I'll be here by the door when you finish. Then we'll go visit the other children." She glanced at my shoulder bag. "Anything good in there? Her father had some ideas about possible gifts."

"Met the man downstairs," I replied, softly patting the bag. "I've got just what she wants right here."

"Good, good." Nurse Candy smiled, then suddenly frowned. "She's a sick little girl, Santa. Give her lots of love for all of us."

"No problem," I replied, slightly reluctant to enter the little girl's room.

What will I see? Can she even talk? Will she know who I am? Maybe she'll be asleep. Maybe I should be as quiet as possible in case she's.... naw, I'm Santa and I should act the part or take off this outfit for good.

I stood tall, sighed and decided that this would be my best showing. Santa would want it no other way. I banged on the door frame and hollered, "Ho, ho, ho, it's old Santa come to see you, Braids, so let the party begin."

I entered the room expecting to see a bedridden child gasping for air and hooked to all kinds of gizmos and gadgets. I was quite surprised. She was in bed all right, but sitting up watching "The Flintstones" on an oversized color TV fastened to the wall in front of her. Cartoon characters of every description laughed and played on the remaining walls. There was Bugs Bunny eating carrots. Even the curtains were adorned with Mickey Mouse, Donald Duck, Pluto and the entire Disney entourage. The nurses on the floor had done an exceptional job of brightening up this room. The aroma of freshly baked pizza filled the room.

A muffled giggle came from behind a plain white curtain that partly blocked my view. I could see only her feet, covered with pink bunny slippers.

"Ho, ho, ho," I said again, this time not so loud.

"Is that you, Santa?" a little girl's voice spoke. "I've been waiting for you."

Her voice wasn't what I expected—she had a British accent. I stuck my head around the curtain. "It sure is honey. Say, I'm looking for a little girl named Braids. You're not her, are you?"

She adjusted a homemade knit cap covering her head. "It's me, Santa. I'm Braids. It's really you, isn't it?"

My heart cried from within when she held out her thin little arms for a hug. I stared for a few seconds, thinking about the beauty before my eyes. No frowns, no tears— Braids gave the world no indication of the gravity of her illness. Seven years old at most, she was grinning ear to ear. I held back no longer and rushed to her side, giving her a Santa's hug that was firm, yet soft and gentle. Tears welled up in my eyes but I wiped them away before she could see.

"So," I began, clearing my throat, "how is my little Braids doing today? You look very pretty in those bright red PJs. You're not trying to take my job, are you?"

"Oh no, Santa. Mommy said you would like seeing me in red. You do, don't you?" A worried look flashed across her face.

"They look great, darling. Say, I have an idea. You hurry up and get well and I'll take you for a ride in my sleigh. I think you and Rudolph will hit it off just fine. He likes red too."

"You think so, Santa? I'd love riding to the North Pole."

"You've got a deal kiddo. Get yourself well and I guarantee we'll take that trip."

"What about Joey, my little brother? Can he come too?"

"Why sure, little one. We'll take the whole family if you like."

The loving smile on her dimpled chin begged for a kiss. I gave her one before perching on the corner of the bed. Needle marks dotted the pale, transparent skin of Braid's arms. She leaned back against the pillow, her energy draining quickly and noticeably.

"Shoo, I get tired pretty fast, Santa. I sleep a lot too. Do you sleep a lot since you're so old?"

"Old!" I said indignantly. It was an act and she knew it. "Why I'll have you know I'm only..." I covered my mouth and blurted out my age.

"Gee, that's old," she said, nestling forward on her elbows. "I don't think I'll get that old, Santa."

The eyes of an angel looked into mine, and it was as if she knew what was coming soon. I could not talk, only look into those sky blue eyes of hers and wish I had the gift of healing.

Why the children? Why the children?

I placed my hand over hers. "Say, I almost forgot what I came for. Wasn't there something special you wanted for Christmas this year?"

She placed a thumb in the corner of her mouth, trying not to grin. My goodie-bag lay at my feet. I asked her to grab the rope and help me pull it to the bed. A little reluctant at first, she pulled harder as the edge of the bag came into view. With an extra tug, it was lying on the bed. There was something very special in there for her and she knew it.

"Well now, Braids, let's see if the elves did as I asked and put something special in here for you."

She stared at the bag without blinking. "Gee, I hope so, Santa. Did you get my letter?"

"I sure did darling." My hand slid slowly inside the bag and I wiggled it a few times for special effect. Her request had not been for dolls or other things most girls desire. No, she was unique. Based on my experience I'd say she was one-in-a-million for not requesting a cuddly toy. I pulled out the first gift.

"Wow," said she, her voice up an octave. "You did get my letter. A Monopoly game."

"That's what you requested isn't it?"

"It is, it is!" She turned the box all around and gave it careful examination. "Santa, how come it has a K-Mart sticker on it?"

"Ah, my goodness," I said, showing embarrassment. "I didn't want you to know. Donner, one of my reindeer, wanted a Monopoly game and I had only one left." I looked around the room acting as if I did not want a soul to know what I was about to say. "Don't tell anyone," I whispered, "but sometimes I have to pick up certain gifts when I'm on my run." I smiled, giving her a wink. "I stopped at K-Mart before I got here so I'd have that special gift you wanted. You don't mind do you?"

All curiosity left her face. "No Santa, it was nice of you to do that for me."

"I shop at local stores more than you know, little one— more than you know." I reached in the bag and retrieved another gift, wiggling my hand harder this time. "Say, this little guy doesn't want to come out. You'd better grab my arm and give a tug."

In a flash, she had hold of my arm and was tugging with all her might. As my arm slid from the bag I made an oinking noise.

"A pink piggy!" She squealed with delight. Any passerby would have thought she was as healthy as a horse by the excitement in her voice. "It's a piggy bank." She hugged it like a doll.

"You didn't think I'd forget the most important thing you wanted, did you?"

She said nothing as I slowly slid my hand back inside the bag and pulled out ten rolls of wrapped pennies. I placed them on the bed before her.

"Oh my." Her voice softened as she picked up a roll. "There are so many. There must be a thousand dollars here." She immediately opened one of the rolls and began putting them in the pig, one by one.

"Not quite that many, sweetheart, but there's enough to keep you busy for a while."

"I love coins," she said, not taking her eyes off the pig while stuffing the pennies in the slot.

Slowly, inconspicuously, I placed the bag back on the floor. It was one of the most precious moments I've had, watching that little girl happily stuffing pennies in a pig without a worry in the world. I almost forgot the circumstances surrounding my visit.

"Twenty, twenty-one, twenty-two," she counted as she added pennies to the bank, giggling each time a coin hit the growing pile. She was happy for now and that was important, but I couldn't help wondering how many more giggles remained before her laughter would be silenced forever, at least here on earth. I bowed my head, trying not to show my sadness. The count of fifty brought me back to reality.

"They're all here, Santa. I've been collecting pennies all my life and sometimes I get a package that has one missing. One time I got a pack that only had forty-eight."

"Well, you've got nine more packages to go. How many do you think that piggy will hold?"

"A lot," she said, holding the pig to the light for an inspection. "A lot more."

Suddenly Braids put down the pig, took hold of my left hand with both of hers and looked around to make sure no other ears were listening. "Did you bring it?"

What could I say, I was lost. "Did I bring what darling?" Concern about missing a gift brought a bead of perspiration to my forehead. "I brought what you wanted, didn't I?"

"You brought me everything I asked for, Santa. You can give me the special gift now. Mommy told me you would. It's OK."

I hesitated momentarily, my mind in a spin at the possibility I'd forgotten something. But what? For an instant I flashed back to only a few minutes earlier when I met her father.

Maybe he slipped something into my bag, something that was meant for just this moment.

I sighed, clueless, certain that there was nothing left in my bag for Braids. Our eyes locked as if nothing in the room existed except the two of us. "You know, Santa," she said, "the key."

"The key... uh, you mean...." I looked at the doorknob searching for the answer.

She sighed, exasperated. "Mommy told me all about what might happen soon. She told me you would give me the key." She squeezed my hand. "You know, Santa, the key to the gates of heaven."

I was so stunned I could not speak for several seconds. My heart raced and I felt slightly woozy, but all I could do was sit there. I had no answers.

A television or movie actor playing Santa dons the red suit, stands before healthy children and passes out gifts with grace and composure. But I was facing reality, not a scripted scene. This seven-year-old angel knew her time was limited, and all she wanted was a key to eternity.

What to do. What to do.

My brain searched for an answer, but a blank stare was all I could muster. A Santa's greatest challenge is to deliver that jolly smile while the pain of heartbreak pounds in his chest like a hammer. Most who wear this suit know those feelings. My eyes watered so badly the room was a blur.

Suddenly I had a vision of what to do.

The grin on my face turned genuine as slowly, very slowly, I pulled my goodie bag back upon the bed and reached inside without taking my eyes off Braids. I made no fake movement this time. It was not necessary. Again, in slow motion I pulled my hand from the bag.

Oh Lord in Heaven let this work. It has to, it just has to.

When my hand appeared from the bag it held an invisible key. Was it really there? I sure hoped it was. Opening my palm, I held out the key for Braids to take. It was now or never.

Take it darling. Take it, take it—it is yours!

For what seemed like an eternity she looked at my hand, then at me, and again back to my hand. Her eyes widened as she grinned with glee. "Isn't it pretty, Santa!" Then she caressed it while glancing quickly around the room. "We don't want anyone to think we're crazy, do we?"

"Uh, yes, you're right." I moved my hand closer to hers. "Maybe you should hide it somewhere... like under your pillow would be a good place."

She picked up the key one-handed, still examining it. "Kind of heavy. I think it weighs as much as a whole bag of pennies."

I watched with interest as she took the key and pretended there was a door between us that needed unlocking. First to the left, then to the right, she turned the invisible key several times. Then she pulled the key from the lock and inserted it again, over and over.

"Works OK to me," she said, gently placing the key under her pillow for security. Leaning forward, Braids placed her arms around my neck and gave me a hug. "Thank you Santa," she whispered in my ear. "This has been my very best Christmas."

I hugged her too, and kissed her cheek. She seemed tired and quite weak, probably from the day's routine of shots, chemotherapy and medications. Gently I eased her back against the mattress, the hidden key safely beneath her pillow. She rubbed her puffy red eyes, yawning. It was my time to leave.

"You get a good night's sleep, sweetie-pie," I smiled. "I'll be back now and then to check on you, so keep those spirits up or I just might get upset. Is it a deal?"

She rubbed my sleeve, yawning as her tired eyes fought to stay open. "Santa, thank you for the key. I feel safe now." Her eyes closed while she spoke softly one last time. "I won't use it till I have to."

Chapter 2

Key to the Gates of Heaven

Part 2

I stood just two doors down from Braid's room, completely drained of energy. The only thing keeping me on my feet was the laughter coming from the room. A door blocked my view of the children inside. I was contemplating my entrance when a hand thrust a soft drink a few inches from my nose.

"I thought you were about ready for something cold, Santa."

Behind that icy drink was the face of Nurse Candy. "Ah, what a relief," I sighed. "You're a lifesaver, Ms. Candy. I truly am parched. You know, wearing this suit, it's hot, really hot. I perspire like an athlete when I've got it on." I took several long swallows. "You read my mind—been drinking Coke since I was a kid."

I handed her the empty can and noticed that she was dragging a large box filled with wrapped gifts. "Would you look at that?" I grinned. "Wasn't it nice of old Santa to drop off all these toys for the kids."

15

"You think you can pack all these gifts in that bag of yours?" she asked.

"Not a chance," I replied, grabbing the top of the box while opening the door with my free hand. "Santa brought them this way and that's how they're being delivered." I opened the door wider. "Remember, Nurse Candy, we agreed I get a half-hour with the kids—no parents, nurses or doctors, right?"

"You sure you can handle them all?"

"Trust me, I got something planned not even the children will believe."

"All right, Santa, have it your way. But, if there's any problem just yell."

"Yes, yell," I nodded. "Believe me I'll do just that."

"By the way, Santa," she said, "you did really well with Braids."

I didn't say a word, just nodded. With the goodie-bag slung over my shoulder and pulling the box of gifts, I entered a room slightly larger than Braid's. No pictures adorned the walls, nor was the room furnished with beds. Empty paper plates and cups were scattered across the top of a folding table off to one side. Apparently, the room was used strictly for gatherings. The sickening odor of chemical cleaners hung in the air. At least the children had been fed a good meal before my arrival.

Through the gap between my beard and bangs I sighted seven children, all lined up in a row, boys to the left and girls to the right. All were around six or seven years of age and gave no sign of the demon disease they battled daily.

Chairs lined the wall but no one was seated. A young girl stood before a wheelchair, holding tight to the armrest for support. It was a humbling sight. If necessary, they'd probably have crawled to the North Pole to see me.

Somehow I needed to muster a huge amount of energy if I was going to pull this off as planned. I would accept no alternative. This show needed to be as good, maybe better, than the last one. Not just one, but seven children anxiously waited.

With my lungs filled, my thirst quenched, and lots of toys in tow, the time was right for the show to begin. "Ho, ho, ho," I hollered. "Are all you little monkeys ready to come and say hello to Santa?"

First silence, then mayhem as six excited children rushed to my side. I patted some on the head and gave kisses to others. The seventh child, the little girl with the wheelchair, rolled over and gave me a grin, a hug and three cupcakes she had saved for the reindeer. The boys were more interested in the big box I was dragging.

"Whoa there, little ones, we will get to that later," I said in my most authoritative voice. "Now, here's what we'll do. I want everyone to go back to their seat and I'll sit down over there," I explained, pointing to a spare chair. "All of you can come see me one at a time. Is that OK with everybody?"

Everyone nodded except one boy, who held up both hands to be recognized. "Santa, do we get what's in the box or what you have in your bag?" he asked, grinning and patting his tiny foot.

I grinned back and patted my own foot. "How 'bout I let you choose?"

"I want both," he replied, first pointing to the bag slung over my shoulder and then to the box at my side.

"Go ahead and have a seat my little friend. Let me get things set up and we'll figure that out in a second."

Getting a laugh from the kids, I walked awkwardly across the room, grabbed the chair and placed it directly in front of them. I pulled the box of gifts over by the chair and sat down with my bag on the floor opposite the box. Mimicking a construction crane, I extended my arm over the box, grabbed one gift and laid it on my lap. For the first time I noticed that the toys in the box numbered six—a problem for one of the kids that I would have to handle later.

"All right," I bellowed, adding a fake cough and a side-to-side wiggle of my big belly. "We have a choice, kids. You can come up and get your gifts one at a time, *or* you can all gather around and see what's in the secret bag." I pulled the black bag to my lap. Barking softly from beneath my beard, I wiggled my hand under the bag as though something were alive and playing inside. Once again, all the kids rushed me.

"You got a little dog or something in that bag?" one child asked.

"It ain't no real dog," one of the boys answered.

I gave another bark followed by a lonely whimper.

"Santa," the little girl in the wheelchair cried excitedly, "There's no air in the bag. She'll suffocate."

All eyes were on the bag as I moved it up and down. "What do you think little ones? Should I open the bag and let the little thing have some air?"

"There ain't no dog in that bag," the same boy repeated, his eyes betraying concern.

I reached for the tie-rope, fighting off the *deja vu* feeling that came over me. Like little Braids, the children watched intently as I opened the bag. I saw the same curious expression on the faces of all but one girl, who looked horrified. Maybe she thought the dog was suffocating.

My goodness. Braids would surely get a hoot out of seeing these kids watching me open the bag. She'd even be surprised at what comes next.

With all eyes intently staring at the bag, I slowly reached inside and took hold of the little dog.

I pulled it out slowly, leaning back to give the impression that I too was a bit scared. The children held their breath. As the bag fell away, I grabbed it with both hands and did my Frankenstein laugh, which is more amusing than scary.

"I told you it wasn't a dog," said the suspicious boy.

"It's kind of *like* a dog," I replied, turning the soft pillow to show the puppy embroidered on one side.

"Is it a baby pillow?" another child asked, smiling from ear to ear. "Can I hold it?"

I handed her the pillow. "Wait, wait there's something else in the bag." My hand retrieved a solid blue pillow the same size with a Santa picture in one corner. "Anyone have a use for this?"

"I do, I do," the girl in the wheelchair screamed. "Can I have it Santa, please?"

One by one, I pulled five more pillows out of the bag. Some were plain, some patterned, and each had a picture of a little dog sewn on the front. Soon all the children had a soft pillow. I crossed my arms to rest for a few seconds and watch the reaction of the kids. While they played, I scanned the room to make sure everything was in order and my privacy was assured. The door was closed.

"Everyone has a pillow, right? OK everyone," I grinned, "We're going to do something that's a bit out of character for old Santa." The children looked at me blankly. "We're going to play a little game now. First, a question. Raise your hand if you have the answer. What do we do with a pillow?"

A small, dark skinned boy raised his hand first. "I know, I know," he shrieked.

"First tell us your name."

"Lincoln," he responded quickly, flashing a wide smile.

"OK Lincoln—what do you do with a pillow?"

Lowering his baseball cap and looking about the room at his friends, he answered, "You put it under your head when you go to bed."

"Hey, good answer," I countered. I smacked my free hand against my leg and all the children clapped. "There's something else you can do with a pillow. Anyone know what it is?" I looked around the room at each face and no one seemed to have the answer.

"No one has a clue, right? Tell you what, think about it a second. If no one gets the answer, I'll show you." The children didn't notice my hand creep inside the bag and feel for the next surprise.

Suddenly I yanked another pillow from my bag and shook it high above their heads. Everyone stared, not moving a muscle. Looking at their faces it was obvious only one child knew what was coming. He started to take a step backward but it was too late.

"Oh no," he screamed, squinting his eyes and turning away.

"You guessed it, so you get it," I bellowed. My light forward swing scored a bulls-eye, the blow landing as light as a fly on his forearm.

"You got me," he shouted, laughing wildly before returning fire with his own pillow, which hit me on the top of my head.

"Pillow fight," someone shouted. The battle for supremacy was on.

Right away I was deluged with a barrage of blows that sent me reeling to the floor. Luckily no one knocked off my beard or hat. I jumped back into my chair, purposely leaning to one side so the child in the wheelchair could make a hit. Considering her seated position, the blow was powerful. Laughing to the point of tears, she yelled, "I got him, I got him."

Another salvo of pillows struck their mark from all sides. This time my hat landed on the floor—at the feet of Nurse Candy who stood statue-like inside the door. For a few seconds the room was quiet.

"What on earth are you people doing? Has everyone here lost their minds?" She pointed in my direction. "You... you're as bad as these children." It was hard for her to keep a straight face. "Santa, why I..."

"He's not hurting us, Nurse Candy," one voice said in my defense.

"We're having a pillow fight," another spoke up proudly.

Nurse Candy looked at us for several seconds. Bewildered as she was, her expression showed that she was thrilled to see the kids in such joyful spirits.

"I think we've had enough exercise for one day, *children*," she said sternly, taking the pillow from my hand. "Just where did you get these pillows anyway?"

I glanced at my bag of goodies.

"So that's where you got them," said Nurse Candy, suppressing a grin. She examined the pillow and placed it under her arm. "Think I'll keep this one till you leave Santa."

"I *gave* them to the kids, nurse. Mrs. Claus said they can keep them," I winked.

She nodded. Then gently tapping the big box of gifts with her foot, she bent over and whispered, "Don't you think it's about time for these?"

I said nothing for a few seconds, then winked at her again and turned toward the children. "Well kids, we've been caught. It's time we got on with my visit. Besides, I won the fight anyway."

"No you didn't," one of the children countered. The others agreed that I had lost.

One at a time the children came to me with a wish list of toys they hoped to receive on Christmas Day. The usual things were requested— train sets, GI Joe and Barbie dolls— along with some things I was not familiar with. The children were happy in my presence, their daily deluge of shots, poking, and prodding forgotten, at least for the time being.

I distributed the presents in the box. Each was labeled with a name. Only the little girl in the wheelchair had been overlooked. I could find nothing in the box for her. Not a problem. I had something special in my bag—an unopened box of candy canes. She accepted them happily along with the pillow sewn by Ms. Santa Claus.

Just before I left, one petite girl asked me, "Can we do this again next Christmas, Santa? This is the most fun I have ever had."

Looking into her loving eyes, I thought about her question and wondered how to answer. "If it's the good Lord's will sweetheart, you bet we can do it again next year."

Nurse Candy walked me to the door. "You've done a good deed this evening," she said, giving me a parting kiss on the cheek. "I think next year, though, you can leave the pillows at the North Pole."

I bowed my head in reluctant submission, lowering my beard with a tug so she could see my mouth. "As for coming here this evening, it was my pleasure. Call me any time." Like a child telling an innocent white lie, I grinned and added, "As for the pillows, I promise I won't do that again."

Yeah right!

I made another visit to Braid's room before I left the hospital and she got her licks in with a pillow that had found its way back into my bag. Nurse Candy put it there, knowing full well what I'd do with it.

I will never forget Braids, my little angel in the making. Over 15 years have passed and still I think about her lying in that bed, her bald head under that cap, those doll-like eyes smiling at me. She was one of life's wonders.

Braids never used that key to the gates of heaven. Maybe it was a miracle, who knows. Anyhow, the doctors say she is in remission—alive and well as of this writing. Which just proves that you can never count a child out until the Almighty says it is over.

Was the invisible key I gave her that night real? She seemed to think so, and who am I to cast doubt? I just pray that when my time comes, someone hands me a key.

Chapter 3

Debut in Vietnam

A Kentucky chill was in the air when I boarded the jet bound for the Orient. It was the day my oldest daughter was born—not the most thrilling day in my life, though it should have been. I had been in the Army almost a year and had spent only three weeks of leave at home. The thought of going to a combat zone thousands of miles away evoked visions of John Wayne leading the troops on a victory quest with machinegun bullets whizzing by his ears. Yes, in my wide-awake nightmare I stood next to the Duke.

As the jet taxied down the runway, I blew a kiss from the window to my family. Then those polished silver wings carried me aloft to an uncertain future far away.

At twenty years of age who thinks about the future? I certainly didn't until forced to by the life-threatening reality of war. Leaving home for a year, with the possibility of being wounded, maimed or worse, *that* was eye-opening. I admit that the idea of my death, before my twenty-first birthday, scared me beyond belief. Still I intended to keep my commitment and complete my tour of duty with honor. I figured I could handle a year away from loved ones.

From my window I watched the waves rolling toward the west. I stared for hours as puffy white clouds mingled and merged with the water—or so it seemed. I couldn't sleep. In fact, the only good night's rest I would get during the entire tour was on a big jet flying home.

My orders didn't say precisely where I would be stationed for the next year, but I knew that wherever fate placed me I would do my best. Yet something told me that an awakening lay just around the corner. I had no clue exactly what sort of experience it would be, but my inner voice spoke loud enough that I listened and almost looked forward to the unknown.

Cam Rahn Bay, South Vietnam, 1970. Not quite the combat zone I had envisioned. The compound was encircled with barbed wire. Salt water from the South China Sea filled the bay on three sides. A military airport, hospital, post exchange and nightly movies made this duty station the envy of service personnel assigned elsewhere in the country. All those amenities could be seductive until an occasional calling card sent by the North Vietnamese jolted us back to reality. We drew combat pay for a reason, and that reason flew overhead in the form of rocket-launched artillery.

Then there were the sappers, Vietcong infiltrators who specialized in covert activity late at night. The name alone sends a chill down my spine. They moved stealthily through the compound with a satchel charge of explosives, choosing their targets with little concern for detection. Sappers could be male, female, or even children, but their goal was always the same—sudden death and destruction.

Living in this harsh environment, I would never have expected to get involved in bringing Christmas cheer to impoverished village children. When I'd been in the country for a little over a month, my peers decided I should don the wig of old Saint Nicholas and become the giver of seasonal good tidings. (Truthfully, we drew straws and all my friends cheated by making sure that my straw was the shortest.)

"Sorry Santa," my friend Willie said with a phony grin on his face. "You lose and now you get to be Santa for the evening."

"I don't know guys. I've never done this before."

"You'll do fine," another pal whacked me on the back. "Shortest straw goes, you know. Besides I did it a week ago. It's somebody else's turn this week."

"But…"

"Nothing to it," Captain McBain replied, laughing. "If it makes you feel better Specialist, consider it a direct order. Put on that beard and wig ASAP!"

I was standing in the middle of a military motor pool, the equivalent of your local automotive repair facility, with a bunch of half inebriated guys. I figured I could do no worse than the men who'd played the part before. To my credit I was sober, drinking plain Coke.

"All right, all right, I give up," I said, raising my arms in surrender to their persistent demands. "Where's the beard and wig so we can get this over with. And another thing, who's taking me to the village? Not any of you drunks I hope!"

"Not to worry," said Ric, a friend and close confidant. He had greeted me with a handshake on my first day in the compound. "I'll see to it personally that you get to the village in one piece and come back the same way. Will that set your mind at ease, pal?"

"You bet," I answered and shook his hand for the second time.

Ric was taller than me, skinny, and always wore a boonie-cap covered with fishing pins. (A boonie-cap is like an angler's hat, but camouflage green in color.) A handsome young man with a Rhett Butler mustache and wavy brown hair, he was well adjusted to living in the combat zone.

"So!" the Captain raised his voice. "Here's your beard

and wig." He presented it to me as if I were receiving the Medal of Honor.

Stunned, I backed off a few feet. "You're kidding, right?"

"No," an unfamiliar voice responded from a dark corner of the motor pool.

"Who said that?" I asked.

"Never mind," said Ric, taking the items from the Captain and shoving them in my gut. "We've all done it, it's your turn. Think of it as your initiation into the best motor pool at Cam Rahn Bay."

I stared at what were supposed to be the wig and beard— two mop heads tied together by a few strands.

Is this a joke of some sort? They want me to wear this contraption on my head? Why I'll look like a platinum long haired werewolf in a B-rated Boris Karloff movie.

"Get those articles on right now, Specialist! Not tomorrow, now!"

I reluctantly donned the makeshift wig and beard.

"Hip, hip, hooray," echoed through the structure. "You look great," one guy said. "Can I sit on your lap and tell you what I want for Christmas, Santa?" another guy hollered.

I took a short walk to a washbasin mirror. The reflection took my breath away. Before me was the face of a clown, a Ringling Brothers clown with a mop on his head and beard so fake it was hilarious. With a few adjustments the mop-beard looked slightly better, but the hair piece was impossible. It looked like a mop and stunk like one.

Someone stuck a Santa hat on top of my head and I looked in the mirror once again. Well, maybe I could pull it off. The hat drew attention away from the mop. Santa in jungle fatigues and combat boots—I couldn't help laughing.

"I'll give it a try, men." I was smiling, but I doubt that anyone could see it through the mop strands. "I'm as ready as I'll ever be. Let's hope the real Santa doesn't mind a little help this year."

Imagine me, a Santa's helper. Might even be a little fun.

We left for the village in a military truck full of gifts, with me in the passenger's seat "disguised" as Santa.

A cold breeze blew off the bay as we drove across the peninsula to the village. Luckily the guards at the check station were more interested in entries to the compound than they were in departures. The commander had issued standing orders that no one could leave without prior approval, but perhaps the military police knew our intentions and turned a blind eye to our passing. To this day, I believe the MPs helped to make our mission successful. We waved as we left the guard post.

I reflected on the current situation, which seemed more bizarre with each passing minute. Me, a Santa's helper. I had never even met Santa except as a child. I hoped he had a sense of humor, because I sure didn't look like him. I looked like a... naw, he'd understand.

We drove into town on a road made of packed dirt. It was bumpy and I was thankful there was no rain. "Are we almost there guys?" I shouted over the sound of the untuned engine, "my backside's getting sore."

"We're here," Ric hollered from a seat in the covered bed of the truck. "Get ready, Santa, 'cause the kids, they're gonna love ya."

We turned off the main road and approached a group of shacks made from discarded plywood and metal aircraft pallets. A few had cardboard walls and tin roofs. I guessed that these were homes, though I'd seen better dwellings in a hobo's camp. As our vehicle slowed, the kids rushed to meet us. They were dressed in rags.

A movement in the truck's side mirror caught my attention. Another vehicle was behind us. My heart skipped a beat as four men piled out of a jeep and walked our way. I was pretty sure they were the MPs, though it occurred to me briefly that they might be the enemy. Vietcong were known to visit the village at times.

"We've got company guys." I turned, doing what I could to see through the mop.

"It's all right, Santa," Ric assured me. "They're ROKs."

"Rocks... what's a Rock?"

"R-O-K—short for Republic of Korea. They're Korean ground troops, tough guys. You know, bad dudes that the Vietcong thoroughly hate."

"Why on earth are they here?"

Ric crawled out from under the cover of the truck bed, landing on his caboose. "Say fellas, nice to see you." He stood, brushing off the dirt. "I wasn't sure you were going to make it."

Some English was spoken along with a Korean dialect that I did not understand. What I did understand was that Ric had made prior arrangements to have these soldiers escort us. Stepping from the truck, I saw they were armed and realized that the ROKs were our protection for the evening. My mind eased knowing the Korean soldiers were on our side.

The ROKs positioned themselves at strategic locations around us and the kids. One Korean winked at me and the kids. Another smiled. The other two were strictly business.

The kids surrounded me so closely I could barely walk. "What do I do now, Ric?" I asked.

Ric motioned with his hands. "Kind of move to the hooch if you can and they'll follow. Me and the guys will bring all the presents."

I did as requested, glancing over my shoulder as I shuffled toward the nearest structure. The kids followed as if I were the Pied Piper. I felt good considering the circumstances. I was still leery, but wanted to make my act believable. The kids deserved to have a good Christmas, though I knew that their religious beliefs were different from ours.

There I was, sitting on a wooden crate wearing two mops, surrounded by Vietnamese children, all smiling, laughing, and having the time of their lives. I felt elated. They didn't care about my looks. Tonight was their night to meet Santa and they were ready. All of my butterflies were gone along with any inhibition about being a Santa's helper. I confess that for my first time playing Santa, I was having an ever-lovin' ball.

The inside of the home in which we had gathered was about as makeshift as the outside. The living space consisted of one big room with worn, faded carpet covering a dirt floor. The family that lived here had no separate sleeping arrangements, and the furniture was apparently discarded U.S. government issue. The tragedy of their poverty hit me like a freight train and my heart sank for a few seconds. But when I looked around at the excited kids, my gloom lifted. These children didn't know that they were poor.

My very first "Ho, ho, ho" was horrible, and I coughed midway through to hide my embarrassment. At least it grabbed everyone's attention. All ten children rushed to my side, offering hugs and kisses.

With so many little eyes focused on me, it was hard to decide which child would be the first to climb on Santa's knee. That dilemma was quickly resolved when a little girl about five approached and looked me over from head to foot, her thumb in her mouth. She wore a cute one-piece, coal-black outfit that looked like pajamas. Though small, I could see that she was feisty. I nodded, she nodded back, and I motioned for her to come closer. Without a word, she ran and crawled on my knee, hanging on to my faded green fatigue jacket.

I looked into her dark eyes before speaking. "Well now, young lady, would you like Santa to give you a nice present for being a good girl?" I was startled to hear a voice behind me repeating my words in Vietnamese.

"It's OK, Santa," explained Ric. "Mi, the girl behind you, is going to translate what you say." He pointed to the child on my lap. "See, she likes you. You'd better give her something, like you said."

Immediately another GI handed me a wrapped present. "Go on, Santa, she's waiting."

I never handed her the present—she took it and unwrapped it while sitting on my lap. First the bow, then the wrapping paper; one end of the box, then the other. I knew that opening a present was as much fun as the gift itself, so I waited and watched.

Finally, she pulled out a cuddly stuffed Donald Duck that squeaked. She laughed, squeezing and kissing it. Then she cried big tears of joy. No war could diminish the love she felt for that doll.

She planted a kiss on the back of my hand, which brought a tear to my eye. I wasn't the only one affected. I saw the other men sniffling and wiping moisture from their eyes too. I guess none of us was prepared for a three-dollar doll to have such an impact. The little girl turned to Mi, said something, and kissed the doll on the top of its head.

"She says thank you, Santa," Mi translated with a grin. "She also says you are funny looking, but she loves you."

I sighed and hugged the child. "Tell her that I love her too, and Santa wishes her a very Merry Christmas."

After helping the child to the floor, I motioned for the next little one to join me. A boy about six shuffled to within reach and stopped. He was stocky, with ink-black hair trimmed in a bowl shape. I laughed. It was apparent that this young boy was never late to dinner. His mother coaxed him to sit on my knee, but he declined and stood looking everywhere but at me.

I thought about Santa's gravity-defying "magic finger," the one he places beside his nose before rising up the chimney. As a child, I had believed that touching or holding Santa's magic finger would give the same powers to me. I held out my finger and the little boy took hold of it, shook it a few times and giggled.

"Hello partner," I said softly. "My name's Santa, what's yours?"

"Laung," he replied clearly. Obviously he understood English.

"His father is American," said his mother as she straightened the boy's shirt, in disarray from playing. "We go to meet him soon."

Now I could see that the boy's features were vaguely Caucasian. I bent over to lessen our considerable size difference. "Laung. That's a real nice name. You know who I am don't you?"

"Santa... Santa Claus" he spoke, rolling his eyes. "You have presents for me. Daddy told me before he went home that you have lots of toys."

"Have you been a good boy this year?"

"Oh yes, Santa. I do what Mommy says all the time."

"You sure you wouldn't like to come and sit on my lap?"

"No thank you, Santa," Laung answered politely. "I can see you real good." He squeezed my magic finger when he talked.

Behind me, something poked me lightly in the side. I reached back to retrieve a large, beautifully wrapped box. Slowly I moved it to within a foot of the little boy. His shyness disappeared when the heavy box was handed to him, and he wasted no time in tearing it apart to get inside.

Laung lifted the lid to reveal a bright yellow Tonka truck. Given our remote locality, I was surprised to see such an elaborate toy. Whoever donated it would have been pleased to know the gift was greatly appreciated and played with from the second it was opened.

Laung gave me a hug and a chocolate cookie. The rest of the evening produced memories that I cherish to this day. My mop-beard fell off as the fifth child received his gift, but at that point no one cared. The children played with their toys and passed them around so that each could see what the other received.

Later, thinking back over my first gig, it struck me as odd that there was only one father in attendance. Maybe the fathers were in the army or at another location. I shudder to think of the last possibility—that they were casualties of the war.

In case you have an itch to know where all the gifts came from, I'll tell you. The answer is rather unique. My commanding officer, Captain McBain, not only had a big heart, he had a father who owned a toy store. The captain had worked long hours in the family business to pay his college fees. I guess the toy donations were a fringe benefit.

Regrettably, I cannot remember the name of the little girl who first sat on my lap. Yet that face, those soulful eyes, that precious innocent stare—those are things I will never forget. She is with me in spirit each Christmas when I put on my suit and play Santa's helper. And if by some remote chance she reads this—yes, my little sweetheart, Santa remembers you.

Chapter 4

A White-Bearded Mystery

The residents of Mojave, California, seldom see snow except during rare winters that are both unusually wet and cold. This was not one of those years. On this particular mid-December night the weather was my friend, except for a strong wind that crossed the mountains and valleys with gusts in excess of sixty miles per hour. The sky was cloudless and a blood moon in the eastern sky reminded me of a Christmas tree ornament hanging in someone's living room.

I wasn't excited about going out on such a windy night, so I took my time arranging my Santa suit in its carrying case. It had become my habit to keep all my gear—hat, belt, gloves, boots—in one place, and to check it before I left for an engagement. Over the years I learned to be thorough about such things. On one occasion I got all dressed up in my Santa garb only to realize that my beautiful well-shined boots were still in the closet at home. It was a nightmare. Since the embarrassment of that night I've never forgotten to perform my pre-flight inspection.

My most impressive piece of Santa gear is the beard. While it doesn't overshadow the beautiful red suit my mother made for me, the beard is special—top quality and quite costly. Strap-on and glue-on beards are used by the majority of Santa helpers. Our defense is reasonable I think: If we grew our own beards and kept them all year long the little ones would think Christmas was continuous.

If anyone is tremendously shocked, be assured that Santa himself thought up the idea of false beards back in the 1890s. Before that decade all helpers had real beards. But changing times created a need for more helpers and some could not grow beards of their own. So around the turn of the century a few of Santa's helpers started using false beards and most do today, me included.

At the time this story takes place I had just received a new $300 beauty from my lovely wife, Annie, who thought my old beard needed retiring. Her gift was second to none, a beard any helper would be proud to display. Little did I know at the time that my new beard would be a part of one of the biggest mysteries I ever encountered.

I couldn't have asked for a better night to do my Santa gig. The gusty winds would present a problem only if I let them. As a seasoned Santa's helper, I knew exactly what to do. I would dress in my suit at home, leaving the hat, hair and beard for the last minute, just before I entered the home where I was to perform.

This particular night I had only one appearance scheduled—at the home of a seven-year-old girl and her younger brother, whose parents had made a donation to a charitable organization that provided Christmas dinners to local needy families. Santa's visit was a reward for their generosity. I foresaw no problems. My one stop would take about 20 minutes, and then I'd return home.

The clock on the wall at home read a little after seven.

"Got everything?" Annie asked. "Don't call from some pay phone expecting me to bring your Santa bag because you forgot it again."

"Not likely this time, darling. I've got it all."

"Which beard you using tonight?"

"The new one you bought me. Makes me feel more like old Santa than any beard I ever had. I think the big guy up north would be envious if he ever saw me in it. He might even shave off his own whiskers if he knew how good this one looks."

"Well, you drive careful, hear me? Windy tonight, Santa. And don't forget to…"

"Forget what? Put the beard and hat on before I go in the house? I only forgot once and it was years ago."

"Like I said, you drive careful. That truck of yours is awful light and I don't want you getting hurt. Think of the kids."

She was right to be concerned. The wind was playing havoc with the shutters on our house and I could imagine how it would rock my little truck side to side. But I was used to driving in windy conditions. In fact, the night might be slightly boring with only one appointment scheduled. Standing in the doorway, I gave Annie a goodbye kiss.

"I'll fix you some brownies, Santa," Annie said before shutting the storm door.

"Eat all you make, Queen" I responded and strolled to my truck.

The streetlight was burned out, but the moon illuminated a spot on the curb a few houses up from where I was expected. Earlier that day, I had phoned Santa to see if his sleigh and reindeer were available. They were not. Sometimes I'm lucky and get to use the sleigh, but on this occasion the reindeer were resting for their future trip around the world. I vowed to try again in a few days. Maybe I'd get lucky. It was always a joy to arrive at a residence sitting atop that sleigh.

I turned off the motor and looked in all directions to ensure that I was alone. A gust of wind blew across the hood causing the truck to rock violently. I thought the glass on the driver's side door would break. It stopped as suddenly as it started.

Through the front windshield I could see the power lines swaying too and fro.

I'm glad those wires are sturdy. If they give, this truck will look like a piece of burnt toast.

A weight attached to the middle wire held fast and slowed the swaying considerably. Another glance around and I felt confident things were safe, the wind gone for now. I attached the beard with an elastic band over the top of my head and around my ears. Checking my reflection in the visor mirror, I adjusted the wig. The hat fit tightly around my head at ear level. The bell jingled annoyingly and I vowed for the hundredth time to cut it off when I got home.

I placed my thin, square-frame reading glasses on the bridge of my nose, lightly brushed the beard and hair with my fingers and was ready for business. With the strap of my big black bag wrapped tightly around my hand, I sprang from the door of my truck.

The chill wind quickly informed me that the snap buttons on the front of my pants were unfastened. I hope no one saw Santa standing below a burned out streetlight fidgeting with his pants. It is quite the feat to fasten snaps with gloves on. My heartbeat up a few notches, I sauntered in the direction of the house. "Ho, ho, ho," I bellowed, testing my voice for robustness. "Sounds great. Now I'm ready for the little ones."

Suddenly a whirlwind caught me completely off guard and blew me sideways into a telephone pole. I dropped my bag of candy canes and reached for my hat, holding it tightly against my head. With my other hand I clutched the front of the red coat to keep it buttoned. Hair from my wig blinded me, flopping viciously across my face and forehead with the sting of a whip.

My hands thus encumbered, the very next second I felt a tug on my chin. "Oh no," I hollered. Too late. The beard was off my face, circling up and up in the vortex of a whirlwind. The bitter chill froze the muscles of my bare chin as I glanced up in horror to see my beautiful, expensive beard tangled by its broken strap in electrical wires twenty feet above my head. As quickly as it came the wind was gone, as if whipped away by the hand of God.

I stood for a few seconds gawking at that beard dangling above my head and desperately trying to minimize the crisis. Maybe I could pull this off without the beard. Maybe the kids would be so happy to see me they wouldn't notice. I shook my head in disgust. What was I thinking? It was the stupidest idea ever—a Santa without a beard.

I contemplated the dilemma. These were young children who probably went to bed early, so time was running short. I remembered that I had an extra beard in my Santa case— a worn-out piece with a safety pin holding the strap in place, but it would work. I hurried back to the truck, leaving my bag of goodies on the ground.

"It has to work," I murmured, opening the door to retrieve my suitcase. The beard went on quickly with the safety pin resting snugly against my scalp and covered by the fur-lined hat. Secure in the conviction that the problem was solved, I grabbed my Santa bag from the ground and trotted to the front door. One last glance at the overhead wires told me that my new beard would be aloft for quite some time. What a waste of hard-earned money. How was I going to tell Annie that I had lost her beautiful gift.

With the bag thrown over my shoulder, I cleared my throat and advertised my arrival with three hard raps on the front door. "Ho, ho, ho," I hollered in my Santa voice. "Merry

Christmas to all, and are there any cookies and milk here for ol' Santa?"

I detected no sound from within for a half minute. Then the door opened to reveal two startled children staring at me open mouthed and speechless. As soon as my visage registered in their little brains, both children started jumping up and down like rabbits on a trampoline. I was pleased. In my helper's heart, there is no greater satisfaction than seeing happy children—and these kids were delirious.

"Whoa there, kids. I can't come in till you settle down. Now lets see, you are..." I pointed to the boy. "You are Danny and this must be your sister Alden." They stopped jumping, staring in amazement that I knew their names. "Has everyone been good this year?"

"Oh yes," the little girl answered enthusiastically.

"Me too," Danny said with the same excitement in his voice.

"Good, good," I said, pushing my way through the door. I spotted an armchair across the room and made my way to it. Everything was working out fine. I almost felt at ease wearing the threadbare beard.

So far, so good.

The armchair almost swallowed me whole. I laid my bag to the side and beckoned the boy to take a seat on my knee.

The parents stood at a distance. One worked a camcorder and the other fidgeted with a Poloroid camera. This was my third Christmas at this particular home. They always served me fabulous brownies, but before I could snack there was business to take care of. I helped my friend Danny take his place on my knee.

"So, I hear you've been good this year. Is that right?"

"It sure is Santa. I want a..."

"Say, slow down a little, partner. Isn't there something you forgot to tell me?"

Danny had fire-engine red hair with a cowlick that stuck

straight out from the crown of his head. His hand combed at it fitfully while he thought about my question. A few seconds passed and suddenly he whispered in my ear, "I love you, Santa Claus. See, I remember."

"Well now, I was beginning to think you forgot who your best buddy was," I whispered back. "I love you too, Danny. Now, what would you like me to bring you for Christmas?"

It was always the same with Danny. I could count on him asking for the latest toys he had seen advertised on television. In addition, he usually wanted something uncommon for his age. His parents had informed me earlier in the day that he liked puzzles—the bigger, the better—of animals, especially puppies.

I leaned his way as he ended his list. "You sure that's all you want? A little birdie told me you've been really good this year. Maybe a new bike, huh?"

"I got a bike, Santa. I do want the puzzles, if that's OK."

"Well uh, I think I've got about everything you asked for. I'll make a special note to get you those puzzles. Dogs, right? I believe I can handle that request."

Danny gave me a hug and a big kiss on the cheek, and I gave him some candy canes from my goodie-bag. Since he'd been exceptionally good that year he got a few extras.

Alden stood to the side shifting her weight from foot to foot. She giggled and gave me a big smile. I noticed she had grown quite a bit during the year and seemed tall for her age. Like her brother Alden had fiery red hair, but instead of his smooth complexion she had a face full of freckles. It took only seconds for her to find a spot on my knee.

"It's good to see you again, Alden. I hear from my elves that you've been a good girl this year. Have you?"

She rolled her eyes shyly to the side. "Yes Santa, I help Mommy clean the kitchen table when we eat. Daddy messes it up."

I looked at her parents to see if the remark had slipped

by—it had not. "That's a good girl. Do you say your prayers every night?"

"I do Santa." She leaned closer. "I say a prayer for you too."

"Is that right!" I cleared my throat. "I'm glad you do."

Suddenly a sharp pain traveled along the side of my head and down my neck. Something was terribly wrong. I gasped, realizing that the safety pin had sprung open and was sticking me in the side of the head. Worse, the beard was starting to slip down my chin.

Oh no, not now.

During my years as a Santa's helper I had never had a beard slip, slide or fall off. Why did it have to happen now? In my mind I could envision the entire humiliating scene. The beard would come off in front of Alden and Danny, their parents would be horrified, and I would be disgraced. In a few seconds all the Christmas cheer in this family would vanish unless I stopped what was about to happen.

I quickly stuck the thumb of my free hand through the hole between the beard and mustache, pushing a wad of the beard-hair into my mouth. By biting down on the hair, I managed to halt the beard's sliding motion and hold it in place. Momentarily saved by this fast reaction, I had a new problem. I could speak from only one side of my mouth.

Alden gave me a bizarre stare. "You look funny, Santa. How come you stuck your finger in your mouth?"

"I got a bad tooth, little one. Bothers me now and then," I mumbled.

"Why don't you go to the doctor?"

"I'm going as soon as I leave here, darling."

"Your voice is changed, Santa."

"I've had a little cold, Alden."

Alden gave me a serious, Shirley-Temple glare. "You need some pills, Santa? Mommy's got a lot of pills. She takes a handful every morning and she told me it keeps her from getting fat."

"Fat," I choked, as a few beard hairs made their way down my throat. I remembered how this little girl loved to talk from my previous year's visit. It was her turn, and broken beard or not I was intent on giving her time to tell me her Christmas wishes.

"So," I said, tears forming from the tickle in my throat. "What would you like Santa to leave under the tree this year?"

Alden pondered the question. "I want a new play kitchen set, some dishes, a Mama Frodie doll, a necklace—you know, the ones you can make at home. You put the beads on a string and tie it. I'd like a puzzle too, but not dogs. I like kitties."

I was relieved when Alden finished reciting her long list. I doubt I could have lasted another thirty seconds before gagging on the hair that was caught in my throat and rubbing against my nose. A hearty sneeze was brewing but with steely resolve I maintained my composure for fear of blowing the beard across the room.

"Is that about all you want this year, honey?"

"Yes, Santa," she grinned, and then gave me that shy look made in heaven.

That was my cue, my signal to depart. I hoped I could leave more quickly than I entered. Ramming my thumb again in the corner of my mouth as an added precaution, I silently willed the beard to stay put until I was out the door. I pulled a handful of candy canes from the bag and handed them to Alden. She immediately sat on the floor and counted them.

I stood, gave a wave to the parents and children and departed without saying another word. The parents probably thought it odd, but I was afraid if I tried to speak I'd choke violently or sneeze with such ferocity the beard would fly from my face, giving new meaning to the practice of show-and-tell. All I wanted was to get out of there, rip off that horrible beard and fill my lungs with fresh air.

I slammed the door behind me, making sure no one

could observe my antics once outside. The beard, hat and wig were off my head in a flash. Thank goodness the stray hairs in my throat came out when that beard went flying. The discomfort from the beard far exceeded the pain of the pin repeatedly scratching the side of my face. I sighed with relief as I strolled slowly to my truck for the short trip home.

What a night. Am I glad this nightmare is over.

I didn't bother to look back at either beard. In truth, I hoped some stray dog would rip the old one to shreds, and I assumed the new one was still tangled in the telephone wires. One thing was certain, neither was going home with me. I climbed in the truck, started the engine and pulled away from the curb, plotting the beards' immediate replacement. Santa was scheduled to be on the road again the following day.

On Saturday morning at about nine, I walked to the door of our country home and looked out. "A real beautiful day," I told Annie.

She sat in her easy chair mending a pair of slippers with toe holes. "What's on our agenda today, honey? You going for breakfast as usual?"

"Let's go together," I suggested with an inclusive wave. "Besides, we need to make a trip to town so I can pick up something."

"Where do you want to stop in town?" she asked.

"Well, uh, I'll tell you when we get there. It's a surprise."

"A surprise you say. Well, I've got a few places I need to go, so if you don't mind I'll drop you off, do my shopping and then come back for you."

What she suggested was fine, but I knew she would figure out my intent when we arrived at the costume shop. Annie took my arm and we headed out the door. We walked to her car, which was sitting in the driveway next to my truck. I worried about the cost of a new beard. Three, maybe four hundred dollars I figured. I did not want another cheap one. No, I wanted a good one like the one I lost.

As I reached for the door handle I noticed Annie staring at the rear of my truck. "What is it?" I asked.

"I don't believe what I'm seeing," she said with a bewildered look.

I stepped to her side and what had captured her attention caught mine. "I don't believe it either. Why, I kicked that thing like a football. How on earth...."

Hanging from the bumper of my truck was the worn out beard, its broken strap dragging on the ground. With a little help from my enemy the wind, the beard had moored by a few tangled strands around the bumper and hung on for dear life.

"Is that how you take care of your Santa gear?" Annie scolded with a sour look.

"No, no," I said, making motions with my hands for the thing to disappear. "You won't believe what happened last night."

She frowned. "Let me guess. You were driving down the road with your head out the window and suddenly the beard flew off, right?"

"Not quite that simple. You see my new beard, the expensive one you bought me—it kind of got blown off my face and landed in some electrical wires. I used my old beard, and it flew away too."

"What? You've got to be kidding."

"Wish I was honey."

"You're sure about that are you?" she asked. "You're the only person in the world something like that would happen to."

I rested my arms across the top of her car. "I agree. Only I could get in a predicament like that."

"So that's why you want to go to town today, to get a new beard?"

"Yep."

Annie stared at the bumper and then at the bed of the truck. "Kind of wasting our hard earned money aren't you?"

"I can't help it," I said, sadly. "Mother nature decided it was time for me to get another beard."

"You don't need a new beard."

"I don't need a new beard?"

"No, you don't."

My temperature started rising. Surely she knew there was no way I could do my Santa gig barefaced. "So explain to me why I don't need a new beard."

Annie pointed to something in the bed of the truck. She shook her head and smiled, "Looks like you're back in business, Santa."

If I had false teeth they would have fallen from my open mouth. At first all I saw in the bed of the truck was the spare tire. Then my eyes focused where Annie was pointing. Directly behind and wedged beneath the spare tire was my new beard, and to my surprise it still looked rather decent.

"I guess breakfast is on me, dear," I said, totally bewildered. "Come on, let's go. On the way, I'll tell you the whole woeful story."

To this day I have no idea how both of those beards ended up in the truck and survived the trip home on that windy night. I have speculated that the entire episode was caused by natural phenomena—a one-in-a-million coincidence. Yet neither beard was in my possession when I departed Danny and Alden's residence. So I still find the whole incident decidedly *unnatural.* Supernatural even, but in a good way.

Perhaps Santa intervened. I have it on good authority that Santa loves a mischievous prank now and then.

Chapter 5

Santa's Hideout

When I was young, I always wondered if Santa really made his annual trip around the world in one night. Maybe he could slow time and move through a porthole unknown to science—a rip in space that allowed certain people with knowledge of time travel to enter on one side of earth and exit on the other. That was my childhood theory, when my only worry in life was what mom was cooking for supper.

Now I know how Santa gets around. Should I divulge the secret of his fantastic mode of transportation? The truth is, anyone with a little imagination can solve the mystery simply by watching television. Santa and some of his helpers do indeed travel highways in the sky in a very big sleigh pulled by eight not-so-tiny reindeer.

Where does Santa rest when weary from travel? Does he travel throughout the world on other days besides Christmas Eve? You bet. His pit stops are with his helpers. He knows where every Santa's helper lives. That's the secret to Santa's longevity and the reason he stays so jolly.

Helpers can't always guarantee his privacy, however, especially when little boys are prowling for mischief, as they were one Saturday afternoon in August.

Annie and I live in a quaint desert dwelling that sits on five acres, with a runway where Santa can land when he's traveling—especially on Christmas Eve. The neighbors, most of whom are elderly, could not care less about the goings-on at Desert Dream Ranch, so named by Annie years ago. I doubt if anyone within a mile or so even suspects that a Santa's helper lives nearby and has been a welcome guest in their homes. The few children who live in the vicinity are always visited by Santa a few days before Christmas.

Seldom do children visit our home. It's not that we are bad hosts; all but a few close friends have raised their kids and are now near retirement. An exception occurred a few years ago when a friend brought his spouse and two sons to visit us.

The boys, five and seven, were typical city kids. When given a large area to explore, they were not about to sit around with the adults. You'd have thought these kids had just been freed from ankle chains. Their feet hit the sand-blown driveway at top speed and they were out of sight in seconds. That's when the fun began.

"Annie," I hollered, "they're here."

"Who's here?"

"Jimmy and his family. Remember, they said they'd be by today."

Annie opened the screen door to the front porch. "I know they're coming today honey. Are you getting old? I'm the one who told *you* they were coming."

"Oh, that's right," I agreed, shaking Jimmy's hand and meeting his wife Anna for the first time. The kids were long gone.

Annie joined us by the carport. "It's great to see you both. It's been too long, hasn't it Jimmy?"

Jimmy agreed and gave her a big hug. "Sorry about the kids, Annie. They're out back somewhere. They said they wanted to find a snake. You know kids." He hugged her again and we headed in the house for refreshments.

Jimmy and I had become friends when both of us were stationed at nearby Edwards Air Force Base. After six years in the Air Force, Jimmy had enlisted in the Army. He was now a member of an elite special forces group, the famous Green Berets, and was stationed on the east coast. The family was in California visiting relatives.

"So what about the kids?" I asked Jimmy as he and Anna rested after their drive from Hemet, two hours away.

"You can't keep their minds occupied. If they're not arguing about something they're plotting what to get into next."

Annie poured lemonade and looked out the door at the boys. "They're so big. I can't get over how tall the oldest is."

Anna agreed. "I think he takes after my uncle Dick. He was the tall one on my father's side."

The boys burst through the door, huffing and puffing. They were thirsty from the desert heat and one pushed the other as they jockeyed for position at the lemonade tray.

"Settle down boys," Jimmy scolded. "You're not at home." He pointed at the older boy, scowling. "Stevie, leave your brother alone. You know what I told you about picking on someone smaller than you."

"He started it," Stevie said.

"No, he started it," Craig countered.

Jimmy gave Stevie a stern look. "I don't care who started it. Both of you settle down like I said."

"Yes sir," was their simultaneous response. They exchanged angry stares and continued to nudge each other as they waited for Annie to pour them a cold drink.

"I gotta go to the bathroom, Mom," Craig announced. Stevie nodded his concurrence.

Anna looked to Annie for direction. "Which bathroom should they use?"

"They can use the back bathroom," Annie said, pointing the way.

Craig headed to the bathroom while Stevie stayed for his drink. It was apparent that Jimmy and Anna were loving parents who knew the value of parental guidance. They disliked harsh disciplinary methods and could manage poor deportment quite easily with a simple glance, a cold stare, or an authoritative I-mean-it voice. I was impressed, and that takes a lot of doing.

I took a drink of my lemonade and chewed on a piece of ice. "I'm doing some cement work today. Matter of fact, I'm about half through. If you don't mind, I'd better finish what I started. That stuff sets up quick, you know."

"Sure, go ahead," Jimmy agreed. His eyes shifted to Craig who had returned from the bathroom and was whispering to his brother.

Stevie set his drink on the counter and hastily headed for the back bathroom. I thought he must have had to go badly. Craig picked up his own glass and gulped his drink, his eyes fixed directly on me. He shifted a curious gaze to his father and then back to me. Some of his drink dribbled from the corner of his mouth.

What's on this little one's mind? Why the sudden shift in demeanor?

I smiled, hoping they had not brought a snake inside and lost it in the bathroom. Knowing little boys, I would not have put it past them.

I finished my drink, stood and started for the door, pulling on leather work-gloves. "I'll be finished in a jiffy, everyone. Say, why don't we order a pizza."

"Can I go with you outside, sir?" Craig asked. He moved closer to me.

"I don't mind if your father doesn't care."

"Can I, Dad? I don't want to stay in the house."

"Don't get under RC's feet... and stay close by."

"How about that pizza, people?" I started out the door.

"You order it and I'll go get it."

Annie nodded. "Let me know when you're close to finishing, and I'll call it in."

Craig and I left the house and walked to my cement mixer. The child beside me kept his eyes glued to my face. First he would squint, than sniff as if trying to detect something in the air. I didn't smell anything unusual. We had just reached my mixer when I heard the sliding front door close.

"That's Stevie," Craig said. "He don't like to stay inside either."

"Is that a fact?"

"Yes sir," he responded, hesitating. "Mr. Goodman, do you believe in Santa Claus?"

Surprised, I turned his way. "Why, yes I do. Why would you ask me that?"

His eyes turned to his approaching brother. "Oh, I don't know. Mom and Dad wouldn't answer me when I asked them."

I looked at Craig curiously. "Maybe they didn't hear you. Most parents I know believe in old Saint Nick."

"Who?" Craig questioned.

"Old Saint Nick. That's another name for Santa. He's known by a lot of names around the world."

"Does he come to see you every year, Mr. Goodman?"

Stevie joined us. Like his brother, he eyed me curiously. I knew something was up, but continued to prepare a load of cement. "Santa visits me and Annie every year," I answered nonchalantly.

"How come you smell like Santa, Mr. Goodman?" Craig asked.

I avoided eye contact the best I could, but the older boy squared off with me, watching my reaction. I kept my eyes on the wheelbarrow below the mixer. "I've heard that before, Craig. I smoke a pipe on occasion and I've heard Santa smokes a pipe when Mrs. Claus isn't around. Guess that's why we smell alike."

"Can I help mix that stuff, Mr. Goodman?" Stevie requested.

"Sure you can." Truthfully, the cement was already mixed but I hoped it would give me time to figure what these two were up to. I explained how to use the hoe to mix the cement. Stevie listened intently, but the younger boy wasn't interested. I could plainly see from his expression that his brain was formulating another question. He shifted his eyes between the house and his untied shoe, never looking up as he shuffled one foot in the dirt.

"Uh, Mr. Goodman," Craig asked, "are there any reindeer around here?"

"We have a few deer in the mountains. I haven't seen any reindeer though. I think they mainly live way up north." I turned to face him. "What's on your mind, Craig? You seem really interested in Santa stuff all of a sudden."

Stevie stopped stirring. "He's always asking questions about Santa, Mr. Goodman." His eyes went to my midsection. "Do you eat a lot of food when it's cold?"

"Yeah," Craig echoed. "Do you?" He gawked at my face and swallowed hard. "How fast does your beard grow?"

"That's it," I said, taking the hoe from Stevie's hand. "Just what's this all about, boys?"

The boys ran behind the carport. Had I scared them? Had I said something offensive? Craig popped his head from behind the tractor, smiling. Stevie followed suit. Relieved that the boys were not upset, I continued my work while thinking about all their questions. I had never visited them as a Santa's helper. Maybe they'd heard their parents talking about my side job at Christmas. I finished my cement work and walked inside to cool off. The boys observed my every move, and I could hear an occasional "wow" from their direction.

I called to Annie from the doorway to order the pizza. Stevie and Craig stayed hidden somewhere outside. Their father had to raise his voice before the boys would enter the house, and they complied only after I was on my way to town to pick up dinner.

Throughout the meal Stevie and Craig concentrated their attention on devouring pizza. Not once did they look my way. Instead they played a slight-of-hand game where one tried to get the other's food without detection. I looked around the dining area for some clue to the boys' earlier behavior. Finding none, I shrugged the whole thing off as unimportant.

With dinner out of the way, we spent a few minutes reminiscing about past experiences, then said our good-byes. Jimmy had a family and a new set of priorities. Raising kids and making ends meet on a military income is a monumental challenge. While it would be quite some time before I saw the entire family again, only a few days passed before Annie heard Jimmy's voice on the phone.

To me, an afternoon delight is sitting in my armchair with an ice cold Coke, some peanuts by my side, and a good John Wayne movie on the tube. You know you're living when you see the Duke swagger through an open door, hat half cocked to one side and carrying a lever action 32-40 Winchester rifle one-handed. Some variation of this scene shows up at least once in most of his cowboy movies. Half asleep and in the twilight of a good dream, my eyelids closed just as the Duke—you guessed it—swaggered through a saloon doorway.

"Santa," Annie tugged on my ear. "Santa, wake up. Guess who just called?"

"I never heard the phone ring," I mumbled, still in dreamland.

"You've been snoring for over a half hour."

I coughed, stretched, and forced one eye open. "Let me guess, your mother called again."

She tugged harder on my earlobe. "Not my mother, it

was Jimmy." She laughed and motioned for me to follow her.

"Do I have to get up?"

"Come on, Santa. I have a surprise for you. Let's see if you're as wise as you think."

I followed her to the back bathroom, stumbling over my own shoes. Our little dog Molly had been playing with them again. "Is this necessary? I mean couldn't you just give me a hint what's going on?"

Annie positioned me in a specific spot in the bathroom overlooking an open bay closet that houses our winter clothes. "Sit down on the toilet," she said, a chuckle in her voice. She was having entirely too much fun.

"The toilet? You brought me in here to sit on the toilet? Losing your mind are you?"

She shoved me gently till I sat back on the toilet. "All right, all right, what's so important that you had to bring me in here and plop me on the throne with my pants on?" I gazed around the bathroom.

"You don't see anything, huh?" Annie laughed. "Take a good look, Santa. There's something in here that explains what we were wondering about after Jimmy and his family left. Remember that conversation, Santa?"

I looked helplessly around the bathroom. "I don't see a thing."

Annie reached into the closet and grabbed hold of the garment bag that covered my Santa suit. One sleeve, its white fur trim clearly visible, peaked from beneath the plastic. Annie held it out.

"That's it, that's it!" I shouted. "That's why the boys acted so strangely."

"Jimmy was laughing so hard when he called, I could hardly understand him. He said they no sooner turned the corner than the kids started yelling that they knew were Santa lived, and it wasn't the North Pole."

"Those kids came in here to the bathroom and...."

"That's right," Annie replied, shaking that lone sleeve. "The boys saw the suit and put two and two together. Jimmy said they told all the kids at school that they found Santa's secret hideout. Even some of the parents called wanting to know where the boys got such a wild idea. Can you imagine that?"

The secret was out. A few hundred kids on the east coast knew that Santa was hiding in Mojave, California.

A wise man once said that everyone influences 218 people in the course of his or her life. If that's true, and I have no reason to suspect otherwise, every child who learned that Santa relocated to the California desert has told 218 others, and each of them will tell 218 more. I fear that in a hundred years no one will remember that Santa's original residence was the North Pole. Time will tell, but I think I'll round up a few reindeer—just in case.

These boys are not Jimmy and Craig (chapter 5), but they look as though they could create at least as much excitement.

Chapter 6

Up, Up and Away

Standing at the doorway of an affluent home in California City, I appraised my appearance. The drive from home was tedious and a flat tire had delayed my arrival. My suit was still presentable, but my hands were dirty from fixing the flat.

I didn't think it would be appropriate to arrive, say a few ho-ho-ho's, and then ask if I could wash up, so I decided to use a garden hose next to the front door. Gloves normally conceal my hands, but I had forgotten them this time.

I positioned the hose between my knees and turned on the spigot. The water pressure was greater than I expected and water splashed everywhere. I turned sideways facing the walkway bushes and scrubbed my hands. To my surprise, most of the dirt came off.

The front door opened and a young boy peered through the glass storm-door. His eyes widened in disbelief at the sight of Santa with water running between his legs. Before I could respond, he started shouting, "Daddy, Mommy, Santa's outside wee-weeing on the bushes."

His words shocked me, but of course that's exactly what

the child saw from where he was standing. What a truly horrible situation. I turned to show him that the water was coming from a garden hose, but it was too late. His father had joined him at the door and they were both gawking at me.

"I uh, had to wash my hands," I said, my voice breaking with embarrassment.

The father's eyes moved to the garden hose held by my knees. "Could have fooled me," he smiled, and then broke into laughter. "You coming in, Santa, or would you like a bar of soap and towel?"

The hose dropped from my knees as I turned off the pressure. I shook the excess water from my hands, dried them against my pant leg, threw the goodie bag over my shoulder and walked through the open door as if nothing out of the ordinary had happened.

A large recliner sat next to a well-decorated Christmas tree. Two store-bought fire logs burned in the fireplace. I stopped in front of the fire for a few seconds, warming my hands. Two children, excited about my visit, stood by the chair waiting for me to take a seat, which I hastily did.

I placed the goodie-bag at my side and made myself comfortable. With the parents taping every move, I lifted the first child onto my knee and set the mood with my usual "Ho, ho, ho." To my surprise, the young man mimicked me with a "Ho, ho, ho" of his own. He was about five and a real cutie, with wide-open green eyes, an air of confidence and a grin that swallowed his face. I thought he'd make an excellent Santa's helper someday.

"So my little friend, have you been helping your mother and father around the house this year?"

"So, my little friend," he repeated, "you been helping your father and mother around the house this year?"

I patted his little thigh. "You have an ear for words I see. Do you plan on repeating everything I say?"

The grin never left his face. "You have an ear for words.

You plan on repeating everything I say?"

"Benny," his mother scolded, "stop that. Santa will think you're a bad boy."

I nodded in her direction, then continued. "Well, Benny, maybe we should find out what you would like for Christmas this year."

Not only did he repeat my words, he phrased the sentence exactly as I had, even pausing after "Well, Benny." I was frustrated. This could go on all night. It's times like this when years of experience come in handy.

"I love games," I said. "So here's a word you can't say—ready?"

"I love games, so here's a word you can't say," he repeated.

"Ready, here we go—supercalifragilisticexpialidocious." An astonished look crossed Benny's face. "Ready, here we go... Supercal...."

That was as far as he got. He tried again to no avail. He stared at me and I stared right back. Then he laughed. He laughed so hard I had to laugh too, along with his older brother, mother and father. Is it hard to outwit a child? It wasn't that time, but I've learned that children with active minds rarely give up easily.

"I can't say that word, Santa. Is it a real word?"

"You bet it is. I doubt that I could even say it again."

He giggled. "Do you know any more funny words like that?"

I kissed his cheek and gave him a hug. "No, no I don't, but I'll have Mrs. Claus see if she can find a few more just for you." I gave a quick wink to the parents. "Now my little friend, where were we. Ah yes, what would you like me to bring you for Christmas this year?"

"I don't know," he answered. "I don't know what to ask for."

I leaned forward. Benny's facial expression told me that

he could not think of a thing. "Maybe I can surprise you this year, Benny. I meet lots of children who can't think of a thing till after I leave. Tell you what, you think about what you would like for Christmas and if you remember before I leave, tell me. If not, don't worry. Put your request in an envelope and drop it in the mailbox addressed to me, OK?"

"You mean that?"

"I do, little one. I get thousands of letters each year. Make sure you draw a small heart in the bottom right corner so I'll know to open it first. We got a deal?" I extended my hand as if to an adult.

He shook my hand with both of his. Without letting go, he took a good look at my beard and hat. "How come you never take your hat off, Santa? Is your head cold all the time?"

I responded by removing my hat and placing it squarely on his head. "A little big isn't it?" I folded up the bottom edge to make it fit. "How's that? Now you can tell your friends that you are Santa's helper."

Benny grinned proudly, revealing a gap where one of his front teeth had fallen out. Then he looked up at the ceiling.

"Did Rudolph and the other reindeer bring you here Santa?"

"They sure did. Why, they're up on the roof waiting for me right now."

"Can you take me with you so I can meet Rudolph, Santa? Mommy read me a book last night and he was in it."

I hesitated a second, gathering my thoughts. This was not a new question, but answering it correctly was the key to keeping inquisitive young minds in a believing mode.

I cleared my throat and noticed that everyone in the room was waiting for my answer. "You want to meet Rudolph, do you?" I frowned sadly. "I wish I could let you meet him this evening, Benny, but there's a problem. You see, Rudolph has a bad cold. I'm sure he would love meeting you but your mother and father wouldn't want you to get sick."

Benny bowed his head in disappointment.

"Here's what we'll do, partner. I'll have him call you when we get back to the North Pole and you and he can have a nice talk. You might even remember what you want for Christmas and you can tell him. How does that sound?"

The grin returned to Benny's face. "I would like that Santa. Will he really call me from the North Pole?"

"I'll see to it personally, Benny. Now give me an hour or so to get back. Rudolph will call you when he's settled in. He's in charge of making sure the other reindeer get to bed, you know."

"You promise?" he asked.

"I promise." The little fellow climbed off my knee and joined his parents.

"Who's next?" I asked, looking around the room and pretending not to see the older boy standing by the tree. "Is there anyone else who wants to tell ol' Santa what they want for Christmas?"

Ignoring my invitation, the young man made a show of straightening ornaments on the tree. He was giving me the cold-shoulder, and I had no problem with that. He believed differently than his brother. I respected his silence and left him to the tree.

My duty done, I grabbed my goodie-bag and retrieved a handful of candy canes from inside. No longer preoccupied with the tree, the older boy scurried to Benny's side for his share of the reward.

With a deep-chested "Ho, ho ho! Merry Christmas to all and to all a good night," I strode to the door, waved to the parents and reminded Benny to expect a call from Rudolph. It was a fine evening and I looked forward to a cup of hot coffee at a restaurant not far away.

The evening chill was relatively mild. In fact, it was rather decent outside. I stopped halfway down the walkway next to the house to admire the beauty of the heavens. A quarter moon shown overhead, stars flickered, and I watched a meteor streak across the sky, leaving its tailings of fire.

Ah, a stupendous night. If only I could hop on a sleigh and...

Peripheral movement caught my attention. I froze, not wanting to give away my position if the visitor was a dog. I turned my head slowly, my face half hidden by the goodie-bag on my shoulder. For a second I thought my eyes were deceiving me. There stood the entire family, looking like they were posing for a portrait—the parents locked arm in arm, outer hands resting on the shoulders of their sons. What were they doing? Surely they weren't expecting to see me leap to the roof and take the reins of my sleigh and reindeer.

Apparently that was it. These people were waiting to see me twitch my nose and spring from the ground to the roof. I couldn't think who was craziest, me for hanging around star-gazing, or them for expecting a game of leap-frog.

Maybe if I act like I'm about to jump to the roof they'll go back inside.

I crouched, flapped my free arm like a wing, then took another peek their way.

The family was completely engrossed in my antics.

What on earth are these parents thinking? Was my act that believable?

I stopped waving my arm, shrugged my shoulders and prayed the parents would realize that I was not going to fly like Peter Pan. Obviously, I wouldn't get two feet off the ground before gravity intervened, so I did the next best thing. With a wave, a wiggle and a boisterous "Ho, ho, ho," I turned in the opposite direction and moved ten feet down the walkway. Surely, they would get the message. But when I turned again they were still standing there like Roman statues.

This is ridiculous. Maybe if I act like I'm having trouble getting to the roof, Randy will get the hint and usher them back inside.

Again I flapped my free arm, the other still holding the goody-bag, and tried to act as though I was having problems with my flying technique.

What would Mrs. Claus think if she saw me flapping like a chicken laying the big one.

"Goodbye Santa," Benny hollered. "Don't forget to tell Rudolph to call me like you promised."

"No problem," I shouted back. "You can bet Rudolph will call and I'm sure Santa's going to want to talk to your father too."

None of them budged. I looked around, desperate for an escape and saw a gate at the end of the walkway. It appeared to access the rear yard. Maybe I could hide back there until they went inside.

I reached the gate, grabbed the latch and turned to wave at the family. When the gate wouldn't open, my feverish yanking was answered by deep growls from the opposite side.

"Don't want to go back there," the father hollered. "Big Joe's back there and he's ornery."

"Don't have much choice now do I?"

Apparently the reality of my dilemma finally sunk in because the father hurriedly led everyone inside.

I was breathing a sigh of relief when Big Joe (I'd forgotten about him) hit the gate like a rolling earthquake. I estimate my trip to the truck took less then ten seconds. Ignition and blast off took even less.

I made a phone call to the North Pole when I arrived home. Rudolph was very understanding and made that call to Benny. The next day I phoned Randy, the father. I wanted to know why he had the whole family watching me outside their home. I'd accept just about any excuse, but I definitely wanted this guy in the hot seat.

"So Randy, old friend. You know who this is, right?"

"Oh yeah, you're Santa."

"Good, good, now that the formalities are over, I'd like to know something."

"Sure Santa," Randy said. "Say, you did a great job last evening. The kids loved you."

"Yes, well, that's nice to hear. Listen I need to know, what were all of you doing outside anyway? I mean, you had me in a tough situation. Did you really expect me to jump up on the roof, holler "Hi-ho Silver, Away" and fly into the night with my sleigh and reindeer?"

Randy laughed. "I'm so sorry, Santa. I didn't mention it, but yesterday was Clara and my anniversary. When you arrived we'd already downed about a quart of Christmas cheer."

"You mean to tell me you two were drunk?"

"Sorry Santa. We finished the bottle not more than five minutes before you arrived."

Now I knew the full story. The parents were inebriated—drunk as skunks. In their condition they failed to realize that a leap to the roof by Santa was out of the question.

I promised Randy another visit the following year, but only after he swore that the beverage of choice on their next anniversary would be soft drinks.

Chapter 7

Tiny the Elf

Part One

We didn't know exactly how tall Tiny was. Over six feet, nine inches was our best guess. We measured his height by the entrance of the local Moose Club Lodge. The door was six feet, six inches on the inside frame, and Tiny had to bend over a full head length when entering. He was the tallest person I ever knew.

Tiny must have weighed 450 pounds or more, but we weren't sure about that either. No bathroom scale I've ever seen would hold up under his girth. With feet like an elephant and fingers that could half encircle a basketball, he was massive and ill-proportioned.

Tiny resembled a huge bear, with legs the size of tree trunks and hairy arms that looked like two sides of beef hanging in a butcher's locker. He was balding, aging, had false teeth, and walked with a gimp from a knee that had been crushed some time back.

When I first met Tiny he reminded me of a bad-tempered monster in some Marvel comic book series—a troll from beneath an old wooden bridge. I never knew his real name. Everyone just called him Tiny. A few years back I ran into a close friend of his who told me Tiny was the oldest—and smallest—of five Wyoming boys. That must have been some family to feed.

They say Tiny was a felon who spent time in prison for manslaughter. I never confirmed that rumor, but I do know that he was once a professional wrestler. The Tiny I knew was a gentle person. He often talked about wrestling and his claim-to-fame charity bout with the now deceased Andre the Giant. When asked who won the bout, he'd crack a smile but wouldn't reveal the outcome.

Most people have a pet peeve or two—a subject that raises their blood pressure and their temper. Tiny was no exception. With him, all it took was for someone to bring up the subject of child or spousal abuse. That theme always caused his back to stiffen and his face to turn red. You could tell he didn't just *dislike* child abusers, he loathed them. He proved that one Friday evening while having a few cold beers at the lodge.

A visiting lodge member who'd had too many drinks started roughing up his female companion. Before local members could intervene, Tiny was towering over the man. It wasn't much of a confrontation. When the man threw a blow to Tiny's big belly, his fist just bounced off. Tiny growled, then shook his head in disbelief that the man would even consider violence against such a massive foe.

Most people expect dinosaur-like movements from a person Tiny's size, but my friend was quick. We all watched in disbelief as Tiny took hold of the man's forearms and effortlessly lifted him into the air. Like Goliath, he stood holding the guy a foot off the ground for about twenty seconds, though it seemed much longer. Tiny whispered something in the man's ear. The guy hung there like a wet noodle, not moving, not speaking—just listening.

That was the only time I saw Tiny in action at the lodge.

However, about a year later I witnessed his wrath again when a brutish father backhanded his own daughter in our presence. For a while it looked like the world was going to have to contend with one less abusive parent.

This particular Christmas was no different from any other. Stores were filled to capacity, children entertained visions of sugarplums and adults were generally of good cheer. As in previous years, the lodge elected to visit the needy with food baskets. This time I was invited to go along so that the children at each home could meet Santa Claus.

My sleigh that evening was a dilapidated old school bus owned by the lodge and used on rare occasions—never by children. There were lots of homes to visit that night and not enough vehicles for the job, so by a show of hands that rolling bucket of bolts was hauled from retirement, refurbished somewhat and christened, "The Contraption."

Something new was added that evening: a Santa's helper's helper in the form of Tiny. Dressed in a vivid green elf outfit, he was as funny a sight as I have ever beheld. Ma Goodman, the seamstress who makes my suits on a regular basis, made the outfit. Only problem was, she didn't make it for Tiny. It was tailored to fit a much smaller elf who assists me at times.

The sight of Tiny's girth in that outfit was hilarious. The cuffs were at his knees and the sleeves were around his elbows. His hat sat squarely on top of his head, its bell resting between his thick coal-black eyebrows. On his feet were cowboy boots. He looked like an enormous out-of-the-jar kosher pickle with feet. I have never laughed harder.

The bus was completely packed with food baskets and enough toys for over a hundred kids. We planned on giving out thirty-seven baskets, and presumed that our toy-load was on the plentiful side. "The Contraption" had an unusable bathroom but it would suffice as a changing room for

Santa once we were on the road.

"After you," the driver said, nodding for me to enter. "Santa should always be the first to climb aboard his sleigh."

Sleigh? A deathtrap on wheels is more like it.

I entered the bus, took my place behind the driver's seat, and watched as seven others joined the entourage. Tiny was the last to board. The children were about to meet the orneriest looking Santa's helper who ever lived.

The bus pulled beside an apartment building as I exited the bathroom wearing everything but my beard, wig and hat. "So fellows, are we at the first stop?"

"Yes," the driver responded, shutting off the engine. "You'll have an easy workout here. This is the only stop we have tonight where there are no children."

"Is the basket ready?"

"Right here, Santa," answered Frank, the trip coordinator for the evening.

Frank was one of those people you meet and feel like you've known all your life. A retired postal worker ("mailman" in his time) in his early seventies with paper-white hair, he was quite spry for his age—still worked out with weights. Frank loved conversation—a real bull-shooter like me—so he and I got along just fine.

I donned my beard and hat and picked up the basket, only to be relieved of its weight by a much bigger hand. "Uh, you going on this run, Tiny?"

"Why not? That's why you people put me in this goofy outfit isn't it?"

I didn't have the heart to tell him otherwise, nor did I have the guts. If the man wanted to join in the fun, so be it.

Does he really know what he looks like in that outfit?

As we headed to apartment six, I wondered what the two of us must look like to other residents. Some closed their shades as we strolled by. A woman sitting in a lounge chair beside her living room window did a double take. A second later, she was out of her chair hollering for her husband who must have been in another room. "It's Santa with some monster," she yelled. I laughed—Tiny did not.

On my third knock, the door to apartment six opened slightly and a shadowed face appeared in a four-inch crack created by one of those cheap chain-latch security gismos.

"Good evening," I said, adding a lousy rendition of my Ho, ho, ho. "I'm with the Moose Club Lodge and we're…"

"What's that thing with you," the woman's voice replied.

"What thing?"

"That shadow behind you—what is it?"

I swallowed hard. "Why that's my elf, Tiny."

"Tiny," she said. "Who'd you say sent you?"

"The Moose Club, lady. I've got a food basket for you."

Tiny stepped into the light. "Yes ma'am, it's a food basket we made up for you. "

The door slammed abruptly, though I doubt anyone can really slam a door that's only open four inches. I backed up a few paces, and the lights in the apartment suddenly went out. Someone even shut off the porch light.

"These people got a problem, Santa?" Tiny asked.

"I guess they don't want company tonight," I said, shaking my head in disgust. We left the basket of food on the doorstep and walked back to the bus.

"I scared them, didn't I?" Tiny commented. "Think I'll hang back a little the next time."

I didn't answer, but I knew he was right. His size and appearance apparently scared the people half to death. I was upset that he had been judged purely on his looks. It was all right if his friends poked a little fun his way. We knew what a big heart he had. These folks hadn't given him a chance.

We made three more stops. At each one, children were ready, willing and able to climb on my knee and issue their Christmas orders. As usual, I had a good time playing my role. The bus would arrive at a residence and I'd grab a basket and a few toys appropriate for boys, girls, or both.

And at each residence Tiny declined to join me. I believe his feelings were hurt, though he insisted everything was fine.

"You know, Santa," Frank informed me, "this next visit is going to be somewhat different from the others. Two little girls, about six and eight, live here. Mother works evenings, and father's one of those guys who work awhile, get hurt on the job, draw a workman's compensation check for a few months, go back to work, get hurt again and so on. You know the type."

I frowned. "Sounds like they'll be having a real nice Christmas."

"They're annual recipients. This guy hasn't had a full-time job in years. The mother, she's a real sweetheart, but the dad...."

I stood, hanging on to the rickety vertical pole next to the driver. "What a shame," I acknowledged. "I just hate it when kids get put on the back burner like that."

"There's more," Frank said, his nose and cheeks reddening. "It's not been verified, but the word is these kids get abused now and then."

"Abused," I said. "This guy's an abuser?"

"I'll be going on this trip with you, Santa," Tiny's deep-throated voice intervened. He was standing in a stooped position with his head resting against the ceiling of the bus and his big hand tightly gripping the bar.

"I, uh, I don't think that's a good idea, Tiny. I wouldn't want..."

"You wouldn't want what?" Tiny said. "I'm going along because I don't want Santa to lose it with this... gentleman." A fake grin crossed his face.

As the bus pulled to the curb, I flashed back to something Tiny had said at the lodge earlier in the week. "As far as I'm concerned," he'd said, "rapist, murderers, thugs and thieves, even wife and child abusers, are the worst. If I were a prisoner with a number for a name, I'd show no mercy to any of those vermin."

The smile on his face now was the same as I'd seen then. Was he telling me something that day? He was surely telling me something now.

"Maybe it would be best if you stayed on the bus," Frank said. He knew Tiny better than I did.

Tiny grabbed the basket and an armload of gifts. "Tell you what, fellows. I'll put this stuff on the porch. What you do with it after that is your business."

I nodded. It was a simple solution. "It's a deal," I agreed. "You have to promise to accompany me at the next home, okay?"

The big man nodded, causing his hat to fall on the seat. Both arms loaded with goodies, he stepped from the bus and walked briskly to the front porch. I followed.

Everything was straight—the hat, the beard. All the buttons on my jacket were fastened, as were the elastic straps that crossed under my boots and attached to the cuffs of my pants. I took a deep breath and knocked hard on the door. I heard a shrill holler and some laughter and felt relieved that the kids were in good spirits. Three more knocks and the door opened.

"Ho, ho, ho," I bellowed. "Is there anyone here who wants a visit from Santa?"

"Well, well, well," a sarcastic male voice answered.

"Ho, ho, ho," I repeated, picking up the goodie basket. "You must be Mr. Adams. And I'll bet there are a couple of little girls here who would like to meet Santa."

"Heard it before fat guy," the man said. He stood in the doorway guzzling a can of spirits, his torn tee shirt damp with dribbled beer.

The sight sent shivers down my spine. Just when I figured this was going to be an easy stop, along comes a boisterous drunken father.

Lord, keep me cool and calm with this guy. I can't lose it in front of the kids.

A few seconds passed and his mouth fired off again. "See you got some grub for us. Least I can do is invite you in."

He took hold of my suit by the shoulder pad, gave a yank and pulled me through the door, leaving a pile of neatly wrapped toys on the porch.

"Say fellow," I said, shocked that a person would act that way with his children present. "There's gifts outside for the kids. We should at least bring them in."

"Daddy," hollered the youngest toe-head. "That's Santa Claus. You shouldn't be mean to Santa."

"Both of you," their father shouted, pointing at the children. "Get on the couch and shut up."

Rarely have I seen a parent deliberately embarrass his children in front of Santa. I shrugged off the man's earlier actions but found it difficult to tolerate his verbal abuse of the children. I tried to control my anger.

"Say fellow," I motioned him my way. "It's Christmas," I whispered. "How about letting the girls have a good night. You know, sit on my knee and tell me what they want for Christmas." I don't think he heard me because he just stared dumbly across the room. "What do you say?" I continued. "There's a lot of nice gifts outside. We can make this a Christmas the girls won't soon forget."

"Gabby old goat, aren't you," he spat, backing up a few feet while taking a slug of beer. "That's the trouble with all you do-gooders. You think because a man gets down now and then, you have the right to come in and run his household." He sent the can, now empty, flying through the kitchen, hitting the back door.

I flinched, not from the can hitting the door but because something quite odd had caught my eye. For a split second a dark shape had blocked the light coming through the window in the back door. I shrugged it off as a flickering porch light.

"Why don't we calm down some, fella. Like I said, it's Christmas."

I decided to ignore him. Maybe he would just go away. I took a deep breath and did a special "Ho, ho, ho" for the little ones. Oh, how they loved it. A passer-by would have figured the house was full of squealing baby pigs. They bounced up and down on the couch and forgot their belligerent father for a few seconds.

"Can we tell you what we want for Christmas, Santa?" asked the oldest with enthusiasm. "Can we, can we?" the other begged.

So far so good. The father had left and gone to the kitchen—to get another beer, I assumed. "Why sure you can tell me what you want," I answered, sitting down in a nearby armchair and casting a wary eye toward the kitchen.

The two girls sat anxiously waiting for my summons. I waved the little one over first. She was reluctant, but when I opened my arms for a hug she snuggled in for a long one. Then she climbed on my knee and sat there staring into my eyes with her thumb in the corner of her mouth.

"So," I said, not so boisterous as to scare her. "What's your name, darling? Now, let me see.... Is it, Jackie?"

She laughed. "No...."

"I'll bet it's Alice isn't it?"

"No...." She blushed, rolling her eyes toward her sister.

"Ah, I'll get it right this time. Your name is... Sheryl Lynn, isn't it honey?"

She gave me a heart-melting smile and replied, "My name is Sheryl Lynn." Then, lucky me, I got another hug.

"Ouch," someone hollered from the direction of the couch. I hesitated to look. I was already hot under the collar, too hot for my own good. It would not take much for me to take matters into my own hands and discipline this beast of a father. I did not care to do so in front of the children.

I looked. Sure enough, there he sat with his arm around his older daughter's neck, pinching her thigh. Suddenly she flinched, and the can of suds slipped from between his legs, draining onto the carpet. He recoiled angrily and backhanded the little girl's cheek while letting loose a barrage of four letter modifiers.

He jumped to his feet and I noticed that his groin area was soaked, whether from the spilt can or his own bladder I couldn't tell. He was a pathetic sight and I wanted to laugh, but didn't. Still, I was at my wits-end with this guy.

I lifted the younger child off my knee and gently seated her on the carpet. I stood, facing the father, the veins in my temples throbbing. Does Santa have a temper? You bet! Especially when it involves children in an abusive situation.

Call the law? Maybe tomorrow. Tonight this person is going to get a lesson in humility from none other than Santa himself.

"Kids," I said firmly, "Santa wants to have a little talk with your father so would you please go to your room for a few minutes." I stared at the man, unblinking. He stared back, though I detected fear in his face, not anger.

Without a word, the children hurried from the room. The second they were out of sight I pulled off my hat, beard, wig and Santa glasses and laid them gently on the chair. For what I had in mind, they would simply be in the way. I envisioned my size eleven-and-a-half, extra-wide foot buried past the ankle somewhere unmentionable.

Why not go for it? If anyone deserves it, this clown does.

I'd dealt with dozens of apparent child abusers over the years, but never physically. All the pent-up frustration of those experiences surged through me. This individual was within seconds of feeling the full wrath of my anger. Was it the wrong thing to do? Maybe, but I told myself that after tonight this father would never again dare to raise a hand against his children.

"Mr. Adams," I said, holding my temper back by a thread.

"I've seen enough to last a lifetime this evening. Striking your child, doing so in front of me, that's the biggest mistake you've made in your entire miserable life." I took off my white cotton gloves and slowly strolled toward the man. "When I leave here tonight you can bet you'll never lay a hand on anyone ever again. You earned it. You deserve it. Now it's time you get my message."

Something caught my eye in the partly open kitchen doorway. I froze in my tracks.

A large green arm protruded through the opening. The finger of an immense hand beckoned Mr. Adams to come hither. I knew what was attached to that massive arm and I knew what would happen if Adams took a walk through that door.

Curiosity filled the small corner of Adam's brain that wasn't soaked with liquor. He looked at Tiny's arm in amazement, then casually strode toward the door.

Should I intervene? Should I issue a warning regarding the unavoidable calamity about to befall this guy? I should.

"Say, Mr. Adams, I'd strongly advise you not to go there. Deal with me. You'll be better off in the long run, take my word on it." He didn't hear a word, just walked forward as if drawn by a magnet.

The door banged open. Tiny stepped inside wearing his ridiculous hat with the bell. He looked bigger than before, and his stony face scared even me. Adams was so horrified he froze, unable to move or speak, though some parts were obviously working because his pants got wetter. Tiny grabbed the man by his forearm, gave me a nod, and disappeared out the door with Mr. Adams in tow.

I wondered what I should do. Tiny, judging by his state of vexation, had watched the man's antics through the window. He was absolutely enraged, a madman by anyone's standards. I only hoped he did not send Mr. Adams to the eternal fires below. I ran to the door to take a peek and make sure Tiny hadn't torn the man limb from limb.

I didn't see anyone so I hollered, "Tiny!" No answer. "Tiny, you out there somewhere?" Still no answer. Surely they were close enough to hear my voice. I cupped my hands over my mouth for another try. "Tiny, answer me!"

The oversized elf in this photo is Colonel Dick Stevens, posing with Santa at Edwards Air Force Base in 1996.

Chapter 8

Tiny the Elf

Part Two

"Santa, Santa," one of the girls yelled from the bedroom. Not wanting to be seen out of uniform, I dashed to the armchair and slipped back into my beard, wig, hat, glasses and gloves.

"Santa," Sheryl Lynn said behind me, just as I finished restoring my fictional identity. "Who is Tiny?"

"Oops," I said, turning to face her. "You're not supposed to know that one of my elves is outside minding the reindeer."

"Where?"

"On the roof, darling, on the roof."

"Where's daddy? Is he on the roof too?"

"Uh, he very well could be by now, honey."

"Is your elf coming in? It's getting cold outside, Santa."

Bobbie Sue joined us. "No honey," I answered. "I doubt it. He's talking with your father."

"Can we tell you what we want for Christmas now, Santa?" the oldest requested.

"Why sure you can. That's what I came here for, isn't it!"

There was nothing more I could do. The contest outside was out of my hands. Part of me prayed that their father was still among the living. Another part of me figured the living would be better off without him. I sat in the chair and helped the youngest to my knee.

While the children sat with me, my eyes continually darted to the kitchen door. They requested the same stuff as do most girls of six and eight. What one wanted, the other wanted. It was obvious the girls cared for one another. Bobbie Sue even straightened Sheryl's overly large britches—hand-me-downs I was sure. They seemed unconcerned about the whereabouts of their father. I guess they had no worries since he was with Santa's elf. Me, I worried for all of us.

Just as Bobbie Sue finished giving me her Christmas list, the kitchen door opened and in stepped Mr. Adams. His appearance was alarming to say the least. The man looked like a ghost. He was the color of a freshly bleached toilet, as white as white can be.

I saw no need for the children to notice their father's pallor. I hurriedly turned them around and kept their attention by telling them a bedtime story about the time Rudolph fell from the roof of a home while scratching at a flea on his backside. I watched their father's head twitch and jerk several times as he stood in the doorway.

Adams' forearms were fiery red where Tiny's hands had gripped them. I could see finger marks wrapped around his arms like rope. I envisioned Mr. Adams hanging by his arms like wet laundry on a clothesline. No other marks were visible, though I could not see through his shirt.

The man stood there twitching for a minute or two. It was tough dealing with all this—keeping the kids occupied and watching their father to see what came next. Finally he shuffled past me expressionless, eyes straight ahead, arms dangling, head twitching with each step. I heard the bedroom door close and exhaled in relief. I hoped that was the end of Mr. Adams for the evening.

No sooner had the bedroom door closed than Mrs. Adams arrived from her evening job at a local grocery store. She was an attractive woman, and I silently questioned her reasoning for staying with that bum of a husband. Her personal feelings were really none of my business so I welcomed her home with a wave and a hearty "Ho, ho, ho." She appeared to be tired, but nonetheless smiled at me and affectionately hugged her children.

"It's nice to see a familiar face around here, Santa." She kissed each child on the cheek. "We, uh, seldom have guests these days."

"Just happened to be in the area, Mrs. Adams. The kids and I needed our yearly talk, so here I am." I glanced at my watch. "Oh my, where's the time gone. Well, I'd better be on my way, lots of other places to visit before Christmas you know."

"Where is your father?" Mrs. Adams asked Bobbie Sue.

"He's in bed, Mommy.

"Yes, yes, I figured," Mrs. Adams said, looking embarrassed.

"Kids," I said. "Time I get to work. Remember, do as your parents say, always, and I promise I'll be good to you both on Christmas Day. A deal is it?"

They nodded vigorously. I rose from my chair, distributed a few candy canes from my goodie-bag, and motioned for Mrs. Adams to come closer.

"You'll find quite a few presents outside on the porch," I whispered. "Be sure to get them after I leave. Your husband didn't want me to bring them in."

"I thank you from the bottom of my heart," she said, her voice quivering slightly. "I knew you were coming this evening, but I couldn't get anyone to trade shifts with me, and I can't afford to miss any time. They don't pay us if we're off." She smiled. "Be sure to tell the members of the lodge that I appreciate everything they've done for us. Things will be better next year. My husband, he'll get back on his feet." She planted a kiss to my cheek and said again, "Be sure to tell everyone how grateful I am."

All was said that needed saying as far as I was concerned. I blew a kiss to the kids and left, heading straight for the bus while removing my top-gear. I wondered if Tiny was on the bus. What was he thinking taking matters into his own hands—entering the house and forceably removing Mr. Adams? Couldn't he see from his peeping-Tom location that I had things under control? Maybe that was it. Maybe he intervened to protect me.

The interior of the bus was dark, but I could see everyone's face in the glow of the street light. Old Tiny sat there laughing. In fact everyone on bus was busting up, as if someone had just told a great joke.

"Am I missing something?" I asked, climbing aboard. They laughed even harder. "So, is someone going to let me in on the joke?"

"Not much of a joke," Frank informed me. "Tiny was just telling us what happened in the house."

"He was, was he?" I studied Tiny carefully. "How 'bout it, big fellow, you going to tell me what went on with you and Mr. Adams?"

"Not a lot to tell," he said, giving Frank and the others a sly nod. "Mr. Adams and I needed a heart to heart."

"A what?" I questioned.

"A heart to heart, a nice long talk about life in general."

I laid my goodie-bag on the seat along with my hat, beard and wig. "Can you be a little more specific, Tiny? Couldn't you see that I had things under control?"

"Under control!" he answered. "Why, if I hadn't joined the party you'd have twisted the man's head off clockwise."

"Well, isn't that exactly what *you* had in mind? And another thing—why did you go get your hat?"

Tiny's laugh echoed throughout the bus. "I wore my hat as a disguise. If he and I meet on the street, he won't recognize me. The hat hides my ugly mug."

I didn't know whether he was serious or jesting. "Come on, Tiny, fess-up. What did you do to Mr. Adams? He came in the house looking like he'd seen the devil in person."

The entire bus rocked with laughter. "You might say he did," Tiny responded. "First thing I did was hang him up by his arms. Then I growled and licked my lips as if I was going to eat him. You know, I think he really believed it too." Tiny paused, wiping the corner of his mouth. "I can't think when I've met such a miserable excuse of a man. The guy was slobbering, blowing bubbles from his nose and he cried like a baby when I..."

"When you what, Tiny?" I demanded.

"When I licked his cheek like a pork chop."

No longer able to maintain my composure, I joined the laughter. Frank was laughing so hard he choked and had to be smacked on the back.

"Go on, go on," I appealed.

"Well there we were, he and I," Tiny said. "I growled a little more, then told him I was sent by the devil to escort him to his new home down below. I said we were proud of him for all the rotten things he'd done in his lifetime. When I told him that smacking his kid upside the head fulfilled the final test for getting into the devil's vacation spot, the guy went crazy—screaming, swearing he'd never do it again and he wanted another chance. If I'd held him any longer his eyes would've popped right out of their sockets. He was petrified."

"Well, wouldn't you be scared if some giant grabbed you by the arms and threatened you with the fires of hell?"

"I'll say," Tiny interrupted. "But Mr. Adams will remember this night for a long time, I guarantee."

"You didn't lay a finger on him, right?"

"The closest I came to harming a hair of his head was when I licked him."

I grinned. "What did he taste like, Tiny?"

"Dead meat, my friends, dead meat."

Frank motioned for the driver to take the wheel and proceed to the next stop. Worn out from my ordeal, I took the seat behind the driver and pulled a Coke from a cooler graciously provided by the lodge. Tiny joined me after things quieted down somewhat. I wondered if our actions would make a dent in the character of Mr. Adams. In most people it would have, but this guy was a real loser in my eyes. I pondered our responsibility toward his family.

"Tiny," I said, sipping my drink. "Don't you think we should maybe contact the authorities in the morning? A Zebra can't change its stripes overnight. The police should know about this guy."

Tiny thought a few seconds before answering. "Tell you what. Before we take that step let's come see him in the morning. We'll know if he's learned his lesson."

"That reminds me. Did you just drop him on the ground?"

"Oh no. The last thing I told him was that Satan had personally given him to me, and that I thought he was real cute for a human. That did it. He started kicking and screaming, and the darn guy's foot almost got me in the groin."

"I believe I've got the picture. You dropped him like a hot potato, uh?"

"That's about it. He hit the ground running like an Olympic track star too. Funniest thing I've seen in years."

I patted Tiny's back. "You're quite the actor. So you think we should visit him in the morning?"

"No doubt in my mind," Tiny said. "We'll be able to tell if he's a changed man by the look in his eyes. And, if I'm wrong... Well, we'll make a little visit to the law Monday morning."

I agreed with his suggestion and dropped the subject for the time being. Besides, we had other places to visit that evening. Under my breath I prayed that the rest of our stops would be uneventful.

Sunday morning at quarter past ten I sat in my truck in the lodge parking lot. Tiny arrived and lumbered to my vehicle for our trip to the Adams home. The weather was mild, but I wore a jacket in case the breeze picked up.

Would Tiny be right? Would Adams be a changed man? I doubted it, but my resolve had softened overnight and I hesitated to report the guy to the local authorities. Of course, I would if it seemed like the right thing to do. Maybe we'd be lucky—maybe he'd skipped town.

"Good morning, Tiny. Have you had your coffee yet?"

"Close to a bucket full I'd say." He piled into the passenger seat, giving the shocks a good workout.

"Sure you want to go through with this?" I asked. "I can't for the life of me believe this fellow's nature is going to flip-flop overnight."

"Drive on, Santa, drive on. I'll show you what this ugly mug of mine can do to a man's will." He wiggled uncomfortably in the seat, trying to arrange his long limbs.

"Sorry pal," I said. "This is the biggest truck I've got."

"Had that problem most of my life so don't worry. I'm used to it, believe me. I was told I weighed fifteen and a half pounds at birth," Tiny admitted. "Mom always said I was going to be big and she was right."

It was a short trip to the Adam's house. Both sides of the street were filled bumper to bumper, so I pulled into the driveway and turned off the motor. I had no idea why there were so many cars. Maybe a wedding reception or overflow parking from the corner church.

The garage door was open and the family car gone, but the front door was ajar so it appeared that someone was home.

"Time of reckoning, old buddy." I opened the door and stepped from the truck. "Come on, Tiny. Let's see if this fellow remembers last night."

"You go," he insisted. "I don't want the kids to see me. I might scare them."

"Don't you want to see how your little visit went with Mr. Adams? Aren't you at all curious?"

"I am. I think I know what you'll find. Don't even want to take a chance of scaring those babies. You go. I'll be fine. Leave the keys in the ignition so I can hear a little country music." He scratched his temple with a grin that said he'd just stolen Grandma's pie. He settled into the seat and signaled good-bye with a nonchalant flitter of his fingers.

Something else was keeping Tiny from going to the house with me. I wondered what it was. The only way I was going to find out if our visit the previous evening had made a difference was to go to the door and knock. Taking a deep breath, I did just that.

Mrs. Adams was a gracious host. For nearly an hour we chatted over coffee and donuts. Then she walked me to the porch and waved good-bye through the storm door. I wondered what she would think if she saw Tiny sitting in the truck, but she didn't notice him.

I chuckled, waved good-bye and headed for the truck, barely containing my excitement.

"It's a miracle," I said, walking around to the open passenger window "Nothing short of a miracle, my big friend."

"So the old boy saw the light!" Tiny laughed, almost choking on his candy bar. "Isn't that peachy-creamy. Completely amazes me how a Zebra can change its stripes overnight."

"You win my friend, you win," I said. "How on earth did you know the man would see the light?"

"Rather not say," Tiny gloated. "Is he home?"

"No. You ready for this? The guy took his kids to church. His wife said she's never seen him so enthusiastic about going to church. And you know what? Mr. Adams is an atheist, a real non-believer."

Tiny tossed the last part of his candy-bar out the window. "I never liked those things anyway. Feed the rabbits, they've got to eat too." He looked my way. "He's an atheist, huh?"

"That's what his wife said. Least he was. Don't you want to know what went on after we left last night? "

Tiny yawned. "Oh yeah, give me the grizzly details."

"All right," I agreed. "But, let's get out of here before he and the kids get back." I walked to the driver's side, climbed in, started the engine and headed back to the lodge. As we drove my mind worked feverishly, trying to put the pieces together. Why didn't Tiny show more interest in what I considered a miracle?

He's holding something back—something secret he doesn't want me to know.

"Mrs. Adams said that her husband was completely under the covers when she entered the bedroom last night. She said he was hysterical, out of his mind. He told her about meeting the devil's own son last night."

"Devil's own son, you say."

"That's what the man called you. He bought whatever you told him, hook, line, and sinker. Said you told him he had only one chance to live a little longer."

"No, I told the clown he didn't have *any* chances left, and that I was taking him with me to that big barbecue down below. They always think they're getting another chance, always."

"What do you mean always, Tiny? You talk like you've done this before."

Tiny ignored my question. "Sorry Santa," he sneezed. "What was that you were saying?"

I returned his sneeze with a fake one of my own. "Never mind Tiny, never mind." I continued driving until we reached the lodge. We entered and had a nice lunch. I related to some of the members how Tiny's oddball tactics had single-handedly changed a man's belief in the Almighty.

Unfortunately, not long after our escapade with Adams, Tiny abruptly left town. Someone from the lodge explained that he was called home to Wyoming to help on the farm. His twin brother—the only one left at home—had been killed in a car accident and his aging mother couldn't handle the farm alone. I missed seeing the big guy. He never wrote, thank goodness. His penmanship was even worse than my own.

One morning I was sitting at the counter of a mom & pop café having coffee with a local police officer. We were sharing stories, and I ended up telling him the entire saga of that fateful evening, including how ridiculous Tiny looked in his elf outfit.

The officer chuckled. "I'd give a month's pay to have been there. Imagine Tiny as an elf."

"What a minute," I interrupted. "Do you know the guy?" I held one hand way over my head marking Tiny's height, and stretched the other hand to the side, illustrating his girth.

"That's him," the officer said shaking his head.

I studied the officer, curiously. "If you don't mind telling me, sir, I'd really like to know where you know Tiny from."

The officer's face became stern. "Tiny is real special in my book," he replied thoughtfully. "I'm not at liberty to divulge any confidential information but I will tell you one thing. Your situation with Mr. Adams was not an uncommon occurrence. We have numerous incidents of child and spousal abuse around here. It happens all the time. Problem is, we arrest these losers, haul 'em in, and they're back on the street before we finish the paperwork. They seldom see more than a day's jail time."

"Go on, go on," I almost begged.

"Tiny was our ace in the hole you might say. He did a lot for the community, though he'll never get the medal he probably deserves." The officer paused, taking a drink of his coffee. "You see, Mr. Goodman, your Mr. Adams wasn't the

Santa Goodman greets a delighted child at a holiday appearance.

Santa with an unidentified helper-elf. "Tiny the Elf" (chapter 7), is one of many volunteers who have worn the green costume.

Santa arrives by fighter jet to greet a throng of eager children at Edwards Air Force Base in California (story, chapter 12).

Above and below: Santa makes his way across the tarmac at Edwards Air Force Base.

Three generations. From left: Robert Clifton Goodman III and Robert Clifton Goodman Jr. holding Robert Clifton Goodman IV.

The author with his father, Robert Clifton Goodman Sr., who wore the red suit in a spirited one-night masquerade (chapter 14). Also pictured is Tinkerbell, who still resides with the author's mom.

first to see Tiny's wrath, there were others, believe me—lots of others. Tiny is the best actor I've ever known."

When I left the café that day I realized that I didn't know Tiny at all. No wonder he knew what the outcome would be that night—his skit was well rehearsed.

As for Mr. Adams, he works a steady job these days at a fast-food restaurant. I doubt that it pays much, but at least he is working and providing for his family. I don't think that he recognizes me when I visit the place. If he does, who cares. He learned his lesson the hard way—but he learned.

A little something I neglected to mention. Tiny was no man's fool. He was an educated man with a diploma on his wall to prove it. However, he seldom talked about his youth or college days. He lived his life his way, and still does I'm told. When people ask me what his degree is in, I tell them, "Psychology, what else?"

Dedicated Santa's helpers know that children, like this boy, may remember their visits with Santa for the rest of their lives.

Chapter 9

The Miracle That Was

"Now I lay me down to sleep. I pray the Lord my soul to keep. If I should die before I wake, I pray the Lord my soul to take. Lord, I know my little brother is with you. He was a good brother. He didn't cry much, as sick as he was. We never got to talk. He wasn't old enough. Mommy and Daddy miss him a lot. I told them you would take care of him. I miss him too, Lord. So if you don't mind would you tell him we all love him. Amen."

I slowly backed away from the doorway of the little girl's room, not wanting to impose on a child's precious moments with God and her parents. Dawn Ann was her name. She was six and doll-like, with ink black hair and striking blue eyes that could melt the hearts of the toughest men I knew. I stood watching in the shadowed darkness as she knelt beside her bed in a pink cotton nightgown to recite her evening prayers. Before crawling into bed, she glanced my way and gave me a quick wink. I didn't think she had noticed my presence—I was wrong.

Dawn was tucked into bed with loving care by her mother, Bess. Both parents gently kissed her cheek. "Go to sleep, my love," her mother said, brushing a few stray hairs from Dawn's forehead.

"One more night, Mommy. One more night and Santa's coming to see me. I've been good this year, haven't I?"

Bess faked a frown. "Well, I don't know—there was that time you...."

Dawn curled forward on her elbows. "I've been helping you cook Daddy's supper every night and I clean my room every day. I vacuumed the carpet in the living room last week."

Bess cast a quick glance at her husband, Tony, who stood silently by her side. She chuckled. "Honey, using your toy vacuum cleaner doesn't count."

The little girl looked at her father who, unbeknownst to Bess, nodded encouragement to his daughter. "Mommy, I think I have been good this year. Santa told me last year that if I keep helping you and Daddy I will get what I want for Christmas."

"What might that be, young lady?" Bess asked.

"Oh, I can't say. It's a big secret between me and Santa."

Bess leaned forward from her perch on the edge of the bed. "Then I guess we'll just have to wait and see, won't we?" Again, she gave her daughter a good night kiss before she and Tony left the room.

I took one last look at Dawn lying in bed. To her left a small rag doll of ethnic design was partly covered by the blanket. On the pillow to the right of her head was a framed photo of her brother, Jose. I had seen this precious child on occasion and held the little fellow in my arms. His premature birth had resulted in complications, including an underdeveloped heart. The spunky little boy astonished everyone with his will to survive. A fighter to the end, Jose passed away peacefully in his mother's arms on Easter Sunday morning at the age of twenty months.

I took a mental photo of Dawn lying in bed, then followed Bess and Tony to the kitchen.

Tony and I sat at the kitchen table having cake and milk, my bonus for being Santa's helper. On many occasions I arrange to dine with the host family prior to my Santa appearance. Of course, during that part of the evening I wear everyday attire.

"So Tony," I said with a sheepish grin. "That little girl in the other room, she's smarter than we think. It won't be long before she figures out who I am."

He sipped his milk. "I'd say you're right, Santa. That kid surprises me with something new every day."

"She sure surprised me earlier this evening," I agreed. "You'd never in a million years guess what she wants for Christmas."

Bess intervened. "I know something she wants—a computer. She says most of the kids in her class have computers at home. They use them at school like we did pencils and paper."

"You're right," I replied. "Education today is a lot different than it was when we were in school."

"Yeah," Tony jokingly responded. "I know for a fact they didn't have computers five hundred years ago when you were a kid."

"I'm not five hundred years old."

"When you put that red suit on you are," Tony said.

"No comment," I said, smashing the few remaining cake crumbs between my fork tines. In truth, I had hardly heard a word Tony said. The picture of that little girl saying her prayers kept flashing through my mind. Worse yet, when I'd talked with Dawn earlier, as Santa, she hadn't asked for a computer. I toyed with the idea of telling this couple her request. Seldom have I passed along any part of a conversation between myself and a child. Strict confidence is the norm. I decided to make an exception in this case.

"Bess," I said seriously. "If you don't mind, stop your kitchen chores for a few minutes and have a seat. The three of us need to have a nice talk and it's about Dawn."

Tony looked alarmed. "Is something wrong? She's not sick?"

"Nothing bad," I said, lightly squeezing his forearm. Bess sat down next to Tony as I continued. "She told me something earlier I thought you two should know."

A hush filled the kitchen, except for the leaky faucet's drip, drip, drip against a frying pan. Bess and Tony's eyes were full of concern. I broke the silence by asking, "Do you two have a clue what she wants Santa to bring her for Christmas?"

"What she wants *you* to bring?" Tony asked.

"Have you seen any other Santas in this house tonight? Yes, I'm talking about me."

Tony looked puzzled. "Well, no."

"I'm here to tell both of you that she didn't say anything about a computer." I paused, gathering my composure. "Dawn asked for a baby brother."

Bess sniffled with surprise. "A baby brother... she asked you for a baby brother?"

Tony squeezed her hand on the table. "I had no idea. We uh... now just isn't a good time."

"You know," I said, fidgeting with the tablecloth, "I talk to a lot of young couples at Christmas. The subject of kids often comes up. I hear the same thing year in and year out. They all want kids—they just want to wait till they can afford them." I grabbed both their hands with mine. "I've learned over the years that if a couple wait till they can afford a child they will never have one."

Bess looked from me to her husband and back again. "It's not a money thing, Santa. Tony's a good provider. It's just that it took us three years to have Dawn Ann. We've been trying to have more children. But you remember the problems we had with Jose."

"Yes, I remember. How could I ever forget! Listen, I apologize for being nosy. I'm just concerned, that's all."

I realized that in my desire to help, I was meddling. It never entered my mind that they had tried, but failed so far, to have another child. While Santa doesn't give his helpers the power to handle fertility problems, he does have superb rapport with the Almighty. I decided that a prayer was in order—a good one.

My cake was gone and it was time to bow out gracefully. I gave Bess a gentle hug, shook Tony's hand and left, still thinking about Dawn.

The bitter cold wind of winter wrecked havoc through the cracks and crevices of my home. Earlier that evening I had tried in vain to light the pilot on my furnace, but it was still out. The three of us—me, Annie and our poodle Balentine—cuddled under thick blankets.

Even the warmth of an electric blanket didn't take away the image of Dawn kneeling beside her bed. Her prayer played over and over in my head like a stuck record. I had said my own prayer while driving home. Maybe it would boost the signal and double the power. While Annie lay fast asleep at my side, I stared into the pitch-black darkness, tossing first to my left, then to my right.

A waste of time, this is a waste of time.

I sat up in bed, yawning, and suddenly flashed back to an earlier incident. My granddaughter, Kaitlynn, was a late arrival because her mother, my daughter Margie, had lupus. Bess had the same disease.

During the time my daughter was having trouble concieving, the doctor's prescription was to take mere aspirin a few times a week. I had suggested at the time that he was a quack in a white robe. Nine months later I ate those words. It worked then, so why not now? A few aspirin couldn't hurt a thing. Maybe Bess should give it a try.

I got up and went directly to the living room phone. The clock above the kitchen sink read ten-forty. Tony was a

John Wayne fan and this was the Duke's night on the tube, so he'd be up all night.

I flipped on a light and found Tony's number on a scratch pad. The wind howling through the furnace ducts sent a chill down my back. Shivering, I dialed the number. That furnace was getting fixed first thing in the morning.

Tony answered the phone in a robust wide-awake voice.

"Hope I didn't disturb you," I said.

"Not at all, Santa. If you're calling about the cake—you ate it all."

"No old friend, that's not why I'm calling. Something's been on my mind. I just couldn't sleep. You got a minute?"

"Sure, why not, commercial time anyway. Fire away."

"I've been thinking, Tony. I don't want to stick my nose in your family's business. What we talked about earlier this evening, I have an idea. May work, may not."

"I'm a little lost," said he. "Give me a hint what you're talking about."

"A brother for Dawn Ann, that's what I'm talking about. I don't know if you remember, but it seems to me a year or so ago we talked about that disease, lupus."

"Can't remember," he said.

"Take my word for it, we did. Anyway, to make a long story short so you can get back to your Duke movie. You are watching the Duke, right?"

"You bet I am."

"As I was saying, we discussed how Bess and my daughter, Marg, have the same disease. There's different types of course. It hit me a few minutes ago. Margie had trouble conceiving and you'll never guess what the doctor prescribed."

"I'm wide awake," Tony responded quickly. "What?"

"Aspirin, good buddy, plain over-the-counter aspirin."

"No kidding!"

"Yes, and furthermore it worked. If you doubt my word I've got a granddaughter to prove it." No sound came over the line. I imagined him standing by the phone in his under-wear, scratching his head. "You still there, Tony? Hello!"

"Sounds a little too simple," he said.

"Did to me too, but by golly it worked. Listen, do me a favor and tell Bess I called. Tell her what we talked about and mention she might discuss it with her doctor the next time she sees him."

"I'll do just that," he said. "Thanks for caring Santa."

"No problem, old friend, just thinking of Dawn Ann. Have a good evening."

I hung up the phone, having done my good deed for the day. Would it work? Time would tell. I felt confident that the Power upstairs had heard my prayers. I was also confident that my boss at the North Pole would do his part.

With a yawn and stretch, I went back to bed. "Good night, Dawn Ann," I whispered. "I have done my best, little girl. And I think we have God on our side."

It was a lazy Saturday afternoon in mid February and I was stretched out on the couch, half snoozing through some lackluster movie. The occasional splatter of raindrops on the roof, remnants of a depleted rainsquall, had relaxed my mind completely. It was the first time since Christmas that the weekend was all mine with no chores to do and no schedule to keep. In a few minutes I would be fast asleep.

The phone rang.

I grabbed the cordless receiver resting on my chest. "Hello," I mumbled.

"That you, Santa? It's me, Tony."

I sat up slowly, trying to force life back into my eyelids. "Tony, give me a sec." I shook my head to get the blood circulating, then gave my face a light smack for shock effect. "Old pal, its been awhile."

"Yeah, well I thought you would be interested to know something."

"Know what?" I responded cautiously, knowing that Tony was prone to trapping people in practical jokes.

"I've got good news and I've got bad news," was his answer. "Which do you want first?"

"Give me the bad news first. This is a joke isn't it?"

"No joking today, Santa. You sure you want the bad news first?"

"Come on, Tony, get on with it. You caught me in the middle of an afternoon snooze."

"Sorry about that. Well, you remember that conversation we had at Christmas? You know, we talked about Dawn wanting a baby brother."

"I remember," I replied groggily.

A painful noise slammed my eardrum. Tony must have banged the phone on his desk, sending a shock wave through the line. "Tony, are you trying to deafen me?"

"Nope, just getting your attention. Bess went to the doctor this morning." he sighed. "Sorry to say, that old stork isn't bringing her a child. Like to have broke her up when the doc told her. Me too."

I shook my head, disappointed that their prayers and mine went unanswered. "It's a shame," I said softly. "The big guy upstairs works in mysterious ways. He's not ready to answer yet. What else can I say?"

"Oh," Tony answered, "he replied all right, Santa. We wanted a baby so bad."

"Gee, Tony, if I could help, I would."

"That's the bad news," Tony said, his voice sounding excited. "Want the good news?"

"Sure."

"My little Bess isn't having *a* child, Santa—she's having a litter."

"She's having a what?"

"Twins," he yelled gleefully. "It's twins. She has two loaves in the oven. Doctor confirmed it a couple of hours ago. Yahoo!"

I was blown away by the news. Sure, I wanted that special gift of life for the family. Sure, I wanted little Dawn Ann to get her wish, a new baby brother to play with, love, and help raise. But twins?

"Have you told Dawn the news, Tony?"

"She was the first person we told. You know what, she didn't act very surprised."

"Wonder why," I said.

"I don't know, but she did say something out of the blue the other day. She said that Jesus and Santa were looking into giving her another brother."

"Isn't that odd," I responded, "a little girl her age coming up with something like that."

"Yeah, well grab your heels, pal. Before I got on the phone to call you, she said she wanted to tell Santa thanks. Said she's already thanked Jesus and she wants to give Santa a big hug."

"I can see where she'd want to."

"No," he said. "You misunderstood me. She wants to see *you.*"

"Me?"

"That's right, she told me to tell you to come over so she can give you a big hug."

In shock, I said my good-byes and hung up the phone. How did that little girl know? Over the years she had paid little attention to me when I visited the family in my civilian persona, and Tony had assured me that neither he nor Bess mentioned my name in conjunction with Santa's. Dawn knew though, or at least suspected.

I looked at my watch. Maybe there was still time to visit Dawn today. I decided to wear my Santa suit to enhance the moment. Feeling great at Tony's wonderful news, I walked to the bathroom closet where my Santa suit waited, covered in plastic. I caressed the white fur around the bottom edge of one sleeve and was overwhelmed by melancholy. This suit had given so much pleasure to kids—if only I could wear it every day. Leaning against the doorframe, I rubbed the fur between my fingers and thought about the miracle of two new lives in the embrace of Tony's deserving family. I couldn't take credit for it, but I knew that my prayers had helped. Joyously, I wept.

Posing for photos is a major part of Santa's job.

Chapter 10

The Boy Who Didn't Believe

There comes a time every year when I have to deal with an unbelieving child. Whether boy or girl, the outcome of the child's entire Christmas often depends on how I handle the situation. All Santa look-alikes have been requested to be on their toes and not to get caught off guard by children with mischief on their minds.

Juvenile delinquents come in all ages, all sizes. Most are intent on disrupting Santa's visit with the other kids. Maybe they do it for attention, or perhaps out of complete disregard for the feelings of their peers. I've seen kids try to pull off Santa's beard out of pure orneriness. Then there are the ones who plainly don't believe.

This story concerns such a child. He appeared to come from a prosperous family. His outfit looked like it cost enough to clothe three kids from working class families. I don't mean to insinuate that well-to-do children are snobby or spoiled rotten. Most are little ladies or gentleman with proper manners. Spoiled is too kind a word for this child anyway. Monstrous describes his personality better.

It happened at a Christmas celebration for employees of a local factory. Every year the company manager made a call to the North Pole and arranged for Santa to stop by the holiday party and meet all the children in attendance. I had visited this particular factory the year before and knew the landscape well, including about how many kids to expect, where to sit and how much time to allot—about two hours.

I arrived an hour early to check out the location where I would greet the children—a stage near the outside door through which I would make my entrance. A stenographer's chair covered in red velvet would be my "throne." Armless chairs are better for balancing anxious, wiggling children on my knee.

Noting no problems, I ate my supper, met a few parents, and then retired to a secluded tool room to prepare for my appearance. The bathroom in the rear of the facility had everything I needed including good light and a mirror.

Dressed and ready for the job, I peeked outside to make sure the coast was clear. My assistant, a woman in her late seventies, stood guard over the tool room door and waved me her way. I trotted to the doorway, stopping for a second to straighten my attire and hoist the goodie-bag over my shoulder.

"You know where to go don't you, Santa?" she called after me.

"Sure do darling." I winked. "Been here before."

It didn't take long for the kids to swamp me. Squealing and hollering excitedly, the little ones, some barely able to walk, clung to my trouser pants like glue. It was a challenge just to shuffle to my chair, but I managed, with all thirty kids at my heels. A horde of parents stood not far from the children, camcorders rolling. High intensity flashes partially blinded me. It was pure luck I made it to the chair.

"Ho, ho, ho," I said again before sitting down. A few kids still had their arms coiled around my legs. "Has everyone been good this year?"

A youngster not more than four unwrapped himself and scaled my torso as if on playground bars. I was not impressed by his lack of consideration for the other children, but he was already sitting on my knee smiling at me with a big pumpkin face.

"Well, little one, I see you're ready to tell old Santa what you want for Christmas."

"Yes Santa," he said in a shy way, grinning toward his parents. "Did you bring me any candy?"

I laughed. "I sure did partner. First you have to tell me what you want for Christmas, then we'll see what's in my goodie-bag for you."

The young boy recited his list, which was somewhat shorter than I expected. Normally when a child is so intent on being first on my knee, his desires exceed the entire stock of Toys-R-Us. But this list was short, as was the next child's, and the next.

The time was going fast, too fast. Experience told me that I needed a shy, reticent child to slow the pace. It took only a second to spot her.

"Who's next?" I asked. I reached down and took the hand of a girl about seven. She stared up at me wide-eyed. If ever I had the gift of intuition, it was with me that moment. This youngster was the perfect pick—totally awe-struck by my presence.

Suddenly a young boy bullied his way to the front. A problem child, I presumed, who did not respect me, this girl, his parents, or anyone else.

"Ouch," the little girl yelled as he elbowed past her tiny frame. Did the boy think I was blind? He now stood where the little girl had been, planning his prankishness. I deal with such children every year but it never ceases to amaze me that a child so young can deviate so drastically from other children. I cringed at the devilish look in his eyes.

"Why, hello there young man," I said as he helped himself up on my knee. I judged him to be about eight. He had exceptionally thick snow-white hair, and seemed cool, calm and collected as he settled in for what I assumed would be a lengthy stay. Though he was well mannered at first, I sensed a mischievous mind behind his red-cheeked face.

"Are you the real Santa?" he asked, smirking as though he knew the answer.

"I certainly am. And what's your name?"

"You don't know my name? If you're the real Santa you should know my name."

I smiled beneath my beard. "Certainly I know your name."

"Then what is it?"

"Now Shane, did you really think I would forget you from last year?"

Surprised, he leaned back and looked at me inquisitively. "You... you do know my name."

"I know the names of all my little children. Oh, on occasion I mispronounce one, but you can bet yours is a name I can never forget."

"How'd you do that? Somebody told you didn't they?"

He was guessing. He couldn't know that earlier, while eating, I had talked to his parents, who now stood by watching with enthusiasm. They also mentioned that he was a beard-puller.

"Isn't that your name?" I queried, raising an eyebrow.

"Yeah, but..."

"Then that's all that matters, right? Now, let's get down to business. Have you been a good little boy this year?"

"Yes I have. Have *you* been good this year?" he asked, his eyes wandering all over my face.

"Oh I'm always good. Mrs. Claus wouldn't let me come and visit all the children if I weren't." I glanced around the room to guage my surroundings.

"Are you the real Santa?" he asked boldly. "Last year Mom took me to see Santa three times, but they weren't the real Santa. How do I know you are?"

I laughed, keeping a wary eye on his hands. "I'm the

real Santa all right."

"Then prove it," he said. "The ones I saw last year had fake beards and I pulled them right off. I'll bet yours comes off too."

An interesting thought came to mind. If this young man pulled the beards off other Santas why hadn't he given mine a big yank? Maybe this was a child who *wanted* to believe.

"So you pulled the beards off the other Santas, huh?"

"Yeah, and they came right off."

"What did your mother and father say about that?"

"They said it was mean of me. I should not do it anymore because it ruins Christmas for the other kids. I told them nobody wants to talk to a fake Santa anyway."

"OK, I'll buy that, Shane. What will it take to make you believe I'm the real Santa?"

"There isn't any Santa! The kids at school told me so." He hesitated, then continued with a stutter. "Santa's for little kids and I'm eight and a half."

"If you don't believe in me why are you here?"

"Because... because mom made me come."

"Oh she did, did she? Well maybe she knows there is a Santa and she thought you might like to meet me this year."

He leaned back eyeing my beard again. "If you're the real Santa your beard won't come off."

"Are you sure of that?"

"Yes. There is no real Santa. If there was he'd have a real beard."

I smiled. What a great opportunity to prove to this young man and the children watching that Santa was real. "Tell you what young man, I'm going to give you a chance of a lifetime, a chance to pull my beard right off my face. Why, you can even wave it at the other kids if you like."

"You really mean it?" he said, bringing his hands together.

"I sure do. But there's one thing you have to think about. What if it doesn't come off? Will you believe in me then?"

He hesitated. "There isn't a real Santa! No one can have a beard as white as yours and it's too long."

I laughed. "That's not what I asked. If you yank on it and it doesn't come off will you believe I'm the real Santa?"

He eyed my beard, his mind searching for an answer. "Yes, I'll believe there's a Santa but..."

"No buts, my little friend. We've got a deal."

The game was now in his hands. He looked all around. The little girl next in line watched intently, her eyes as big as silver dollars. Suddenly with an expression of delight, he made up his mind.

Adroitly, I moved my right hand under the beard, gripping it firmly. I leaned forward slightly so that he could get a good grip on the wavy white locks that hung directly in his face.

We stared at each other for what seemed like ten minutes, each waiting for the other to blink. Finally he reared back and yanked with all his strength. Silence fell on the crowd as everyone gawked in amazement.

I flinched at the boy's strength, almost loosing my grip. My heart skipped a beat. When I realized that the beard was holding fast to my face, I exhaled heavily and relaxed. Was my young friend convinced there was a Santa? I looked into his eyes for a sign.

Suddenly his arms flexed and he grunted and yanked at the beard a second time. Again, I gripped the beard with all my might, groaning like a bear. I felt the boy falling and clutched his shirt in my fist to stop his backward movement. Immediately he released the beard and went limp, eyes wide, mouth gaping and curly red hair mussed from the ordeal. I pulled him back on my knee and combed dexterous fingers through my disarrayed beard.

"That's showing him, Santa," a little girl hollered. "He's a believer now, Santa," another child said. Hands clapped in the background. One parent suggested some persuasive backside action. I ignored the commotion and held my breath, waiting for his next move.

Shane straightened his shirt and rubbed his left eye, removing a tear. He took a deep breath before speaking, but when he did it was all I could do to keep from laughing.

"I... I want a train set, a new race bike with 20 inch tires, an army set with four army tanks, one of those battleship games." He continued for several minutes.

Before he left Shane gave me a big hug and promised that cookies and milk would be waiting for my arrival on Christmas night. He even insisted on writing down his address to make sure I didn't get lost.

That young man has since grown to be a respectable executive with a local bank. When he occasionally sees me incognito on the street, the first words out of his mouth are, "Hi Santa, what are you going to bring me for Christmas this year?"

By now you probably think that these beautiful children are professional models, but they're real kids from regular homes—a few of the thousands I see every year. Maybe it's the joy of the holiday season that gives them that sparkle.

Chapter 11

Deaf Is But a Word

Church bells rang in the nine o'clock hour on Christmas Eve, the night old Santa would arrive. Dressed in my Santa garb, I was doing my part. The night was especially wondrous because in a few hours the birthday of Jesus would be celebrated all over the world. As I sat in the basement classroom of a Baptist church in El Paso, Texas, visions of what was to come filled me with glee. The little ones had dreamed about it all year—a chance to see Santa in person. Oh, the adoring looks and kisses I would receive.

"Are you ready, Santa?" a mother-to-be asked. "They're lined up in the hallway. They know you are here and we can't hold them off much longer." She glanced down the hall at the kids, then shrugged her shoulders. "Sorry, here they come."

I straightened my suit and leaned back in the comfortable big lounge chair provided by one of the families. Behind me a bed sheet hung, neatly covering a not-so-pretty block wall. The colorful king-size sheet served as a canvas for a hand painted image of Santa being pulled in his sleigh by several reindeer including that red-nosed fellow, Rudolph.

No Norman Rockwell, but a good backdrop behind which to store my wares and special gifts.

A throng of children burst through the door like potbelly pigs heading to a meal. Not one, not two, but all forty swamped me at the same time, almost knocking me from my chair. Santa this, Santa that; I want this, I want that. If not for the mothers I doubt that Santa would be around today.

"That's about enough," one mother yelled.

"Line up like good boys and girls," another woman beseeched, her sizable shape a plus as she gently muscled between the children and me. "Do you want Santa to think you've been bad this year?" She waved her hands over their heads, shooing them back.

The kids lined up like privates ordered to attention by a drill sergeant. The room got quiet. The children understood the meaning of obedience and waited their turn without further defiance. No sooner was I seated in my chair than the first child approached carrying a handful of cookies. With all the shouting, shoving, and grabbing there had been no time for defensive action to protect my outfit and I worried that my beard and hat might be askew.

I motioned for one of the mothers to move closer. "Are my beard and hat on straight?" I whispered.

"You look great, Santa," she assured me, patting my shoulder and giggling. "They're all yours!"

Not a child in the room looked over six years of age. The little boy who approached me was about five. He wore a well-tailored suit and a tie with the likes of me stenciled on it. The little fellow grinned, fluttered his eyelids and stumbled, sending cookies flying two feet over my head.

I grabbed the boy before he hit the carpet. Footing regained, his bottom lip quivered with shame.

Quickly I dropped to one knee. "Don't worry partner. You've got more cookies don't you?"

He looked down, shaking his head. "No Santa. I ate 'em."

I bit my lip to keep from laughing. "Ah, it's all right

partner. I'm too fat anyway." I added a "Ho, ho, ho," which brought a smile to his face and laughter throughout the room.

The child's name was Ron. I knew him from my civilian life, though he did not recognize me. His Christmas wishes were typical for a boy his age. Before leaving the stage, he requested that I take good care of his sister, who was also in line. "She's my best friend," he said.

Throughout the evening the children told me their Christmas wishes. Some of the lists were quite long, other children wanted only one or two things. I kept an eye on Ron, and at times allowed him to help me by getting candy canes from my bag for the other children. He was a worker-bee. When his sister was next in line he reminded me of his earlier request.

Ron's sister was an adorable youngster and she spent close to ten minutes on my knee. She wasn't much of a talker, so I coaxed her with candy canes. Sometimes it takes a small bribe to loosen the tongue of a reticent child. She was helped from my knee by her dad and scampered off to play with the other kids.

When I motioned for the next child to join me, a girl about six eagerly ran into my arms and kissed my cheek before settling atop my knee.

"So Susie," I said, making sure that her mother could heard my voice, "I'll bet you're surprised I remember your name."

She stared into my eyes for a few seconds, then turned to her mother, Faye, who relayed my exact words to Susie in American sign language.

Her hazel eyes as wide as quarters, Susie moved both hands in rapid reply and waited for her mother to translate.

"You remember my name. You remember my name," said Susie through her Mom.

"I know all children's names little one. I remember yours most of all." Faye relayed the words almost as fast as I said them.

"If you remember everybody's name, Santa," Susie asked, "how come you don't use sign language?"

I rubbed my long white beard and watched a look of surprise flash across her mother's face. "I don't need to know sign language, Susie. All words come from the heart and I know that language very well." Again, I paused, squeezed her hand and pushed a curly lock from her face. "Why I even know what you want for Christmas this year."

Faye stopped signing and spoke slowly while Susie watched her lips. "She's learning to read lips," Faye explained. "She's a little slow, but she's smart. Once she gets something down she doesn't forget." Faye watched her daughter reply before turning to me. "Santa, Susie says she doesn't know how you could know what she wants for Christmas. She hasn't told anyone yet."

The burden of proof was on me to demonstrate that I had the magic power to read this child's mind and heart. I relish these challenges. First, I took hold of Susie's hand and placed it over my heart. Then I gave a hearty "Ho, ho, ho." Susie mimicked me in a mumbled though understandable voice. Her mother looked surprised.

I lifted Susie off my knee and stood her on the floor. Then I crouched on one knee beside her. "You don't believe old Santa knows what you want this year, huh? Your little friend, Pouchie, went to doggie heaven not long ago, right?"

Faye translated my words. A look of shock crossed Susie's face and her lip started to quiver. I could see that in a few seconds a river of tears would begin to flow and this little angel's heart would break before my very eyes. Not if I could help it… and I could.

"I've got a big surprise for you, darling," I said. Moving to one side, I pulled back the sheet that hid my gift. The gift barked from its plastic cage. Susie heard neither the bark nor the whining that followed, but her mother did, and grinned as I pulled the cage into view. I pushed open the door latch, reached inside and pulled a Chihuahua pup from his confinement.

When he spotted Susie the dog's tail hit ninety miles an hour—it was love at first sight. I've rarely seen an animal and child take to each other so quickly. As Susie and the dog exchanged licks, kisses, and hugs, young Ron joined in to collect his share of canine affection. I backed off and watched the miracle of love unfold.

Did I use mystical powers to figure out what Susie longed for most? Not at all. I knew the parents long before that particular Christmas Eve and I knew the children too. Faye picked out the puppy from the county animal shelter and then called me to plan the whole happy event. I can honestly say that the love of a mother for her daughter brought about this happy ending.

I don't know who gets more excited when I arrive by fighter jet—
me or the kids.

Chapter Twelve

The Jail Break

Christmas on a military installation is no different from holiday celebrations in civilian towns and neighborhoods. Santa's helpers visit families in all branches of the service—Army, Navy, Air Force, Marines and Coast Guard—both domestically and overseas.

On a military base Santa's helpers are often delivered to waiting children in camouflaged tanks, Humvees, Jeeps, or armored personnel carriers. Once I heard of a helper who made his entrance on a self-propelled howitzer, a long-barrel cannon with wheels.

My favorite way of arriving is in a fighter jet or helicopter. I experience a thrill taxiing up to the kids in an F-16 Falcon, F-15 Eagle or C-130 Hercules.

Most people who get to ride in the back seat of a fighter jet are surprised by the experience. Despite a cost in excess of forty million dollars each, they taxi like old west covered wagons, venting earsplitting noise, swaying side to side in the slightest breeze and, when rolling on concrete with breaker-cracks every fifty feet, bouncing like crazy. These aren't drawbacks by any means. I doubt that any spry young person would turn down an invitation to ride in one. Being in the cockpit of an aircraft capable of speeds in excess of two and a half times the speed of sound is exhilarating, even if you never leave the ground.

Packed in the back seat of a lackluster gray F-16 fighter was a thrill all right, but I felt like a hotdog wrapped in a bun. Wearing my Santa suit and harnessed to an ejection seat, the view was great but movement was out of the question. It is a tight fit for a small person let alone someone my size, big belly and all.

We taxied along at twenty miles per hour, rocking and rolling like a ship in a storm. I didn't care. "Kick this puppy into overdrive," I hollered through the cockpit. I wasn't wearing a mask since we were only taxiing.

Suddenly I received my wish. The pilot, a lieutenant colonel, applied the brakes to stop the mighty jet, then blasted off the line like a dragster. The hair of my well-groomed platinum wig flew straight back, and the g-forces molded my body to the seat. The thrust lasted only a few seconds but it was enough to rocket my heart rate to a record high. The roar inside the cockpit was deafening.

We settled down to a normal ride as the huge dome-shaped hanger that was our destination came into view. About three hundred kids were waiting outside, waving, hollering and jumping around—all for my benefit. It was a great moment. Not only did I enjoy celebrity status as a Santa's helper, it was my forty-fifth birthday.

The pilot yelled back. "Looks like you're a big hit this afternoon. You sure you can handle all those kids?"

"Lets give her a try. I've handled more."

At a couple of hundred feet the pilot slowed the plane and the kids could see me better. I began waving vigorously, rocking back and forth and hollering "Ho, ho, ho." Though the canopy was down, I knew the kids couldn't hear me over the roar of the powerful engine. Nevertheless, the show had to go on, so I continued my antics until we parked.

With help from a few of my elves in military uniform, I crawled from the cockpit without appearing overly awkward. The turnout was impressive—I could hardly believe so many people wanted to see old Santa. I briefly turned away from the crowd and made adjustments to my suit so that I wouldn't be embarrassed by a tilted wig or the sight of my undershirt through an open coat.

I strode briskly down the ramp. When I reached the foot of the stairs I was swamped by the children. Walking was impossible with hundreds of tiny feet obstructing my view of the ground, so I shuffled while talking to the kids, patting some on the head and touching as many as I could with my magic finger.

A hundred flashes of light blinded me. Everyone wanted a picture of their child with Santa. My glasses reflected some of the light, which gave me sufficient sporadic vision to find my way into the open hanger and over to my chair. I needed a few minutes of rest.

My eyes traveled around the hanger. The massive block walls reminded me of a whitewashed picket fence in *Tom Sawyer*. Against two of those walls were tables filled to capacity with food. I quickly spotted the pastries, my favorite dish. Then I saw the old friend who had requested my presence that day.

"Hello Bill," I hollered above the roar of the children. (Three hundred children sound more like a million.) "Glad you could make it today," I waved.

Bill waved back, laughing, "Got your hands full it looks like. I'll see you later during the lull, Santa."

"Bring me a drink will you? It was a dry ride coming from the North Pole." Bill nodded, then disappeared among the adults who stood against a wall. The kids encircled me. I took a deep breath, motioned for the first child to come forward, and settled in for a long visit.

After every hundred children or so I took a bathroom break, not because I had to use the facilities necessarily, but because it was the only place I could get some privacy. The kids followed me everywhere.

I was having a great day. With large crowds of children, I almost always see a few sad faces, but this day I didn't encounter a single one in over three hundred kids.

Each year I find that children seem to crave certain toys. A majority of the boys in this crowd wanted toy airplanes. I was not surprised considering where I was. Numerous kids requested a ride in Santa's sleigh, and several said they'd prefer an F-16 like the one I arrived in.

I sighed with relief and exhaustion as the last child took his place in front of me. The tall, good looking boy had a slight case of acne on his chin, a gift from approaching adolescence. He wore a long sleeved shirt the color of a Washington apple, the shirttails tucked neatly inside well creased trousers with bulging front pockets.

Wonder what's in his pockets? Sure hope it's not a frog or something.

He sat down on the edge of my knee. Since his pockets weren't moving, I figured I was safe for the time being.

"So tell me young man, have you been good this year?"

The boy frowned, his head hanging in a discouraged manner. "I've been good, Santa. I didn't have any other choice."

"Is that right," I replied, patting him on the back. "Well, I'm sure somebody's glad you were good." I looked him over once again. "Haven't we met somewhere? You remind me of someone. What's your name partner?"

"Bret."

"Bret what?"

"Bret Sewer."

I scratched my chin. "Seems I know you, son. I never forget a face."

The young boy squinted. His eyes had a far-away look. "I, uh, I saw you last year at my mother's house, Santa."

Something odd about this child. His mannerisms, his speech, even his facial expression didn't fit the festive occasion. "Now I remember," I lied. "It's your teeth. You had braces on last year didn't you?"

He frowned. "I didn't have braces last year, Santa. I've never had to wear them."

Slightly embarrassed, I decided it was time to end the charade and get on with business. I didn't want to conclude my day on a dismal note, so I offered a ritual "Ho, ho, ho" and whispered in Bret's ear: "Want to take a ride in that F-16 I pulled up in?"

That changed his demeanor real quick. "Can you really do that, Santa?" he asked, smiling from ear to ear. "My dad tried to get some colonel to let me sit in the cockpit of a fighter, but he said no." Bret's eyes met mine. "How did you know that's one of the things I want this year? I haven't told anybody."

"Ah, it's my job to know, Bret." My curiosity aroused, I asked, "You say your father didn't have much luck getting you into the cockpit of a fighter jet. What's your father's name, partner? I might know him."

"Wilber Snodwiggler's my dad. He's not here today."

That woke me up. "Wilber Snodwiggler? Can't say I've heard that name." I paused, trying to figure out what was going on. I knew this boy, but from where? It was those eyes. "Why isn't your name Snodwiggler?"

"My parents are divorced. We changed back to my Mom's name before she was married."

"We, who's we?"

"It's just me and Mom. My older brother was killed in a car wreck and we don't know where my sister is. Mom thinks she ran off with some crazy guy who drives a beer truck."

This was turning into one of the most bizarre stories I'd ever heard from a child. "Sounds to me like you need a good friend, Bret. But it also sounds like you'd enjoy crawling into the cockpit of a jet fighter. Is there anything else I can bring this year that might make your holidays a little brighter? Maybe a new bike?"

"There is one thing you can do, Santa."

"What might that be Bret?" I hugged him closer to let him know I was his friend.

"I want you to help me get my dad."

"Your dad? Where is your father?"

Bret shook his head, staring to the ground. "He's in jail, Santa."

Breath caught in my lungs. What a lousy time for a sad-luck story like this. Worn to a frazzle, numb with exhaustion after dealing with three hundred children, I was ready to go home. Besides, I had no answer for the boy. What did he want me to do, break his father out of jail for the holidays?

"You're father's in jail," I spoke softly. "I'm really sorry, but there are some things Santa just can't do, Bret." I gently nudged him from my knee and turned him to face me squarely. "If I could, I'd help."

"I've got it all planned, Santa. We can get him out of jail tonight. Don't you want me to be with my dad on Christmas?"

Obviously relief was needed. I scanned the hanger and spotted my friend, Bill, visiting with two ladies. A wave in his direction produced no response. Bill was preoccupied but I felt as though he was ignoring me.

I swallowed hard. "What is it you want me to do, Bret? Tell me about your plan." I was wishing for that drink Bill had promised me earlier.

"Let's you and me break Dad out of jail," Bret said, his eyes darting side to side to make sure no one was listening. "We can…"

"Whoa there young man. What you ask is out of my

league. I mean, not that I wouldn't do anything to see that you have a great Christmas. Do you really want Santa to break the law, maybe hurt someone, maybe get hurt?"

"It's easy, Santa. Only you and I will know who did it," Bret grinned. "He's on the second floor and all we need to do is tie a rope around the bars of his window, hook it up to your sleigh and let the reindeer do the pulling. Those bars will yank out easy and dad can ride home with us."

I raised my hands prayerfully, hoping for an intervention. I was too tired to think straight. "Got it all figured out, do you Bret? Did it occur to you that the police might not like us tearing up their jail? And I doubt they would be very happy about your dad breaking out."

"That's what I want for Christmas, Santa," Bret said, standing. "If you can't help me then you're not a real Santa. I'll do it myself if you won't help. Can I borrow the sleigh and reindeer?" Suddenly, he poked me softly in the belly with his index finger.

I stood up. A song in the distance caught my attention.

A number of adults were walking toward me. At first I thought they were moving in the direction of a group of kids playing on an exercise mat that covered a large portion of the hanger floor. Ten people, fifteen—I quit counting when I reached twenty. Some of the children joined in and were singing with the adults. I wondered why.

"Happy birthday to you, Happy birthday to you, Happy birthday dear SANTA... Happy Birthday to you."

I was dumbfounded. How did these people know it was my birthday?

Bill stepped from behind the group holding a huge chocolate cake with a Santa etched in the icing. Another longtime friend, a retired master sergeant, appeared beside Bret and gave him a big hug.

"Hi there, Santa. I see you've met my son." Lonnie laughed along with everyone else. "Did you figure out how to get Mr. Snodwiggler out of jail?"

I looked hard and long at Bret. His last name was not Sewer, nor was it Snodwiggler. His last name was Smith and he had his father's eyes.

"Young man, you mean to tell me you made up that sob story?"

"Sorry Santa, Dad made me do it," he laughed.

Several people shook my hand, personally wishing me a happy birthday. "I can't believe we got you so good," Lonnie exalted. "You don't remember Bret do you?"

"I can't say as I do. I must be exhausted because I seldom forget a child's face."

"I'm joking, Santa. You've never seen him. He's been with his mother since our divorce eleven years ago."

"Eleven years ago?" I peered at the boy. "How old are you?"

"I'll be thirteen next month, Santa."

Lonnie patted me on the shoulder. "His baby-face got you. Sorry pal, we couldn't help ourselves."

I frowned. "You mean all of these people knew about this charade?"

"Yes. We've been planning this for months."

Everything fell into place. Bret had been simply a player in a one-act show called "Get Santa." Bill and Lonnie were the executive producers.

I changed to street clothes and joined the crowd in the break area to keep the party going—eating cake, drinking punch and shooting the bull with my friends.

Later that day Bret's other Christmas wish was fulfilled. He sat in the front seat of a fighter jet.

Chapter 13

The Child Who Knew Me

A friend at work requested that I make my first Santa appearance of the year at his home. I was looking forward to starting the evening with pizza, cold beverages and the company of friends before metamorphosing into Santa. But I was troubled by the weather. This particular winter was especially cold, wet and windy.

The agreement was that Annie and I would arrive an hour before show time and have supper with the family. Then I would retire to the back porch and change into my Santa garb. I was proud as a peacock of my new Santa suit, and could hardly wait to get going. At least the snow flurries were not expected to accumulate overnight.

"It's almost six," Annie called from the kitchen of our cozy country home. "We told Gary and Linda we'd be there no later than six-thirty. Are you ready?"

I pulled my rolling accessory tote to the kitchen door-way, the Santa suit slung over my arm. "Can't we get another carrier?" I complained. "This handle is designed for a short person."

"We'll go shopping tomorrow," she said, finishing the

dishes. "I need some curtain material for the bedroom."

"Sounds good to me," I replied, noticing that she was rather dressed up for the occasion. "A little overboard aren't you? We're only having pizza you know."

Annie flashed her famous mind-your-own-business look and snapped, "Would you have me go in a potato sack? You are not the only one who gets dressed up for the holidays, Santa."

I grinned sheepishly. She was right. Why should I have all the fun? I glanced at the wall clock over the stove. It was time to depart. Annie grabbed the handle of the tote and we left the house. As we walked to the car, I wondered about Gary's eighteen-month-old daughter, whom I had never met. She probably did not talk yet, leastwise not enough to understand. I would soon find out.

The front wheels of our 1979 Toyota Celica slid sideways on the black ice. Fortunately I was accustomed to handling vehicles in extreme situations and on iced-over streets. I just hoped we would not encounter an unusual amount of road grime. Rarely during my Santa career had I missed an appointment.

The home was quite modest and in need of a coat of paint. A cracked window in the door was held together with duct tape, as was a side pane in the living room window. I reminded myself that it was their castle.

"Knock on the door," Annie said, giving me a nudge.

"You think the baby's awake?" I brushed a few snowflakes from my nose. "Do you think my suit will be all right on the back porch? I sure would hate to have some cat take up residence in it."

"The door, Santa," prodded Annie impatiently. "I can smell that pizza from here."

After a few raps the door opened and we were greeted by Gary, who was supporting the baby on one hip. He had definitely *not* dressed for the occasion. A baseball cap covered his slightly balding head, an oversized sweatshirt concealed his watermelon belly, and his trademark faded blue jeans had holes in the knees.

"Hope you two are hungry," he said, getting right to the basics. "There are two extra-large pepperoni pizzas on the table." He kissed the little girl's cheek. "And did you know? Santa is coming tonight."

I tripped on the entrance rug and grinned foolishly, my gaze transfixed by the curly brown locks and big dimpled cheeks of Gary's beautiful daughter. "Can you talk yet little one?" I asked softly.

Gary closed the door. "Not a word yet. I'm still waiting to hear "Da, Da" and it's a bit discouraging."

"Give her time, partner, give her time." I scanned the room and looked down the hall. "Say, where's Linda?"

He frowned. "Sorry to say, Linda got called in to work. We can sure use the overtime pay, but it's a shame she's going to miss Sheila's first date with Santa."

I took off my coat and helped Annie with hers, placing both on a rack behind the door. "Is Sheila still crawling?"

"Flat-out terrorizes the house," Gary countered, handing the baby to Annie. "She runs like a race horse, especially when it's diaper time."

Annie sat on the couch holding the little girl. "She's gorgeous, just gorgeous. And Sheila is such a beautiful name."

"She's named after my grandmother," Gary explained.

Annie coaxed Sheila in a round of patty-cakes. "I'll bet she knows everything we're saying. Look at her smile."

The baby could not take her stunning green eyes off of me. I tested her comprehension with a question I ask all of my young fans. "Do you like candy canes, Sheila?"

Annie sat the baby on the edge of the couch. She promptly slid to the floor and took off down the hallway in a wobbly run.

"Sorry Santa," Gary shrugged, "she just doesn't understand." He placed a hand over his heart in a joking manner. "My poor heart. If she's like her mother, once she does start talking she'll never quit."

We had a good laugh at Linda's expense.

The baby ran wild for the entire two hours we were there. Up the hall, down the hall, around the kitchen table a dozen times, into the living room—the child was a ball of energy.

At times Sheila would stop at my feet and stare for a few seconds, then hit the trail again. On one occasion she dropped her diaper on the living room rug and romped through the house naked with her father close behind.

Around seven-thirty, Santa arrived with his bag of goodies, a robust "Ho, ho, ho" and an invitation for Sheila to come and sit on his knee. In most instances I'm unable to entice so young a child to approach me, let alone sit on my knee. I am sure it has something to do with my appearance in the bright red suit with a beard covering my face. But when I sat down at the kitchen table, Sheila was on my knee before I settled in. Not a whimper, not a tear, and not a bit of encouragement needed.

Sheila tilted her head and looked curiously at my beard. Her tiny finger gently swirled some of the hair. We played patty-cakes while I tried to coax a word or two from her. She was simply not ready to talk.

When her bedtime grew near, Gary took Sheila from my lap and carried her to the bedroom. He thanked us for the visit and promised to deliver a set of snapshots.

After using the bathroom to return to my normal clothing, I passed by the baby's room. She lay cuddled with a teddy bear, and I felt serene in the certainty that this child was content. She was adored by her parents and I knew they would see to it she had a great Christmas.

The months went by and May arrived. On a Saturday afternoon when Annie and I were out for a relaxing afternoon drive, Annie suggested that we stop by Gary and Linda's for a quick visit. I agreed, remembering the little girl continually staring at me during our Christmas visit. "Do you think the baby will know me?" I said. "You know, as Santa?"

Annie looked at me in surprise. "How can that child remember you? She couldn't even talk."

"Well she sure gave me some odd looks."

"You're not in your Santa suit now. She won't know you."

"I guess you're right. But there was something odd about that child," I mused. "Nothing bad, it was the way she looked at me. It's as if she was looking right through me. And she wasn't the least bit scared like most kids her age. Yea, something different there."

"You're imagining things, Santa. She's no different from any other child her age. You'll see." Annie motioned for me to pull into their driveway. "We can't stay long. I have some sewing to do. Lets say our hellos, make sure they're doing fine and then be on our way."

"You mean jump in the car and take off! That's not very sociable."

Annie folded her arms. "That's not my intention and you know it. You're too gabby and I don't want to sit around and listen to all that train stuff you and Gary talk about all the time."

I pulled into the driveway and turned off the car engine. She was right. Gary and I always got involved in lengthy discussions. This time I would tone it down somewhat and not digress about steam engines, cabooses and what railroad company has the most boxcars.

We exited the car, walked to the front door, and were immediately greeted by Linda. Holding the door open, she beckoned us to come in for a visit.

"Hi you two," she said. She was wearing a white nurse's uniform on her tall frame. A little three-cornered hat was woven into her hair, and she looked quite pretty. "Hope you don't mind. I just got off work and haven't had time to change."

Straightening my shirt, I noticed the house had recently been painted. "Is Gary around?"

"He's in the garage working on some old junk car he bought for work."

"And where is the third member of this family?" I asked.

"Sheila is in the kitchen having dinner. I'll get Gary. By the way, I'm awfully sorry I missed seeing you guys at Christmas. I got called to work"

"Yes, we understand," Annie said sympathetically. "Everyone has to make a living."

After a few seconds Linda invited us to the kitchen to see the baby. I sprinted along behind her, eager to see the child. I expected a face smeared with baby food, but to my surprise Sheila sat in a high chair daintily breaking the crusty edges off a tuna salad sandwich.

"She loves tuna," Linda explained, wiping the child's mouth. "Don't play with it honey," she scolded lovingly. "Your daddy won't like it."

"Where is Daddy?" Sheila asked, before taking a big bite out of the middle of the sandwich.

"He's in the garage. He's coming in to give you a big kiss if you eat all your food. And don't play with it."

Gary entered the kitchen through a sliding back door leading from the garage. "Well hi you two. What a surprise."

Linda looked up at Gary while wiping a few drops of spilt milk from the baby's tray. "I was coming to get you in a minute."

"I heard them drive up." He walked to the baby and gave her a kiss on the cheek. "How's Daddy's little pumpkin? You eating all that sandwich?" He roughed up the top of her hair with his forearm as she took another bite.

"Gary quit doing that," Linda said in a demanding tone. "I just combed her hair. Besides, you have grease all over your shirt. Now leave the baby alone and go clean up."

He walked to the sink still making eyes at the baby. "So what brings you two by today? You're not doing your you-know-what this time of year."

"No, no," I said, moving to a chair in front of the baby. "We were in the area and thought we'd stop by and see Sheila. She's talking like a real champ isn't she?"

The baby shifted her eyes to me. She stopped chewing completely and set her milk cup down on the tray. Gary said something and so did Annie but I didn't hear a word because my eyes and the baby's were locked. She pointed directly at my nose.

"Santa," she hollered, "Santa."

"Who's Santa?" Gary intervened, stepping between us.

"That's Santa," Sheila cried again, leaning to the side to see around her father. "Santa, Santa."

All of us were dumbfounded, me most of all. No one spoke for a few moments. I stared at the baby and she at me. The others stared at each other.

What force is working here? There's no way this child could recognize me without my beard, hat, hair and suit. She couldn't even talk when I was here in December.

An unease settled over me. I leaned forward without taking my eyes off of her. "Honey, I'm not Santa."

"You are Santa." Her bright eyes opened wide. "Candy canes, Santa!" she said, holding out both arms while opening and closing her tiny hands. The smile on her face showed absolute conviction. She was looking directly at her own house-calling Santa Claus.

With the cat out of the bag so to speak, what else could I do but concede. I moved closer to collect a hug and a slobbery kiss on the cheek. My identity was not so concealed after all, at least not this time.

Gary informed me the following day that Sheila had watched my every move after Annie and I left the house. She ran to the living room and climbed onto the couch to observe us through the front window as we departed. For the next half hour she sang a one-word concerto: "San-ta, San-ta."

How did the child know my identity? Though I will never know for sure, I do have a theory. It was the eyes. She was able to recognize me by my eyes, independent of other features or my attire.

Today I look at children in a different light because of my encounter with Sheila. Children who are not able to talk understand a lot more than we give them credit for. They process and retain information that they are not capable of expressing in words. That should give us pause.

A little one, wide-eyed with wonder

Chapter 14

The Day My Father Was Santa

A few nights before Christmas Eve, my father briefly became a Santa's helper. It was an accident. He had no training, not even a courtesy call from the North Pole. In fact, Santa never knew about this episode, mainly because I was uncomfortable mentioning it even during casual conversation.

The suits worn by helpers are required to be equal in quality to the beautiful red velvet suit that Santa wears. Years ago, when I was first accepted into the Fraternal Order of Santa Helpers, mine was rented. It was beautiful but it did not belong to me. That's another of Santa's secrets—some of his helpers wear rented suits. Mine was tattered from repeated use—actually, worn out is more accurate. I used the suit proudly but nervously, worried that it would fall apart in the presence of children, an unforgivable eventuality in Santa's eyes.

When the season ended I had the suit dry cleaned and returned it to the costume shop. The sleeves had completely unraveled and the crotch was worn through. Truthfully, I was plain lucky that year.

I promised myself that the following year would be different. I would purchase a brand new suit, the best I could afford.

Thumbing through a costume magazine, I gasped at the astronomical prices. The least expensive Santa suit was $399, and the prices ballooned all the way to $1575. Everything was out of reach—I had budgeted only $250. I worried about what to do for several days until I happened to be discussing the problem in a phone conversation with my mother.

"Why darling," she said. "Why would you spend that much money on a Santa suit? Don't you remember I made all of your sister's cheerleader uniforms while she was growing up. I'll be more then happy to make a costume for you."

Knowing this was the deal of a lifetime I jumped on it, thanking my mother for her offer. Unfortunately, when I mentioned my personal seamstress to other would-be Santa helpers, they wanted her address and phone number. I eventually gave it to a couple of close friends and mother made suits for them at cost. However, of all the suits she crafted mine was by far the prettiest.

A few weeks later my mother phoned to let me know that the suit was ready. She informed me, however, that I would not be the first to wear it. My father had deemed it his responsibility to check the fit and in so doing had spent several hours masquerading as a Santa's helper.

It happened on a brisk evening during the second week of December. On went the pants, coat, belt, boots, beard, white gloves and hat. Dad wore the costume around the house for a few minutes and then marched right out the front door. My bewildered mother wondered if the old man had lost his marbles.

No one had greater Christmas spirit than my father. Every year he transformed their small-town home into a fantasy worthy of Santa himself. Strings of multicolored holiday lights outlined the porch and hung throughout the yard—in trees, on poles lining the driveway, and anywhere else Dad could stretch an extension cord. In the center of this dazzling array stood a life-size Santa in a sleigh with reindeer, Rudolph's nose blinking like a beacon.

My big-hearted father walked into this setting and was literally transported. For the first few minutes he just stood on the porch adjusting to the limited visual field created by the beard and hat. Considering that Dad was only five-nine and weighed one hundred and sixty pounds, and considering that the suit was made to fit my frame— six feet and two hundred thirty-five pounds—I can only assume that he resembled a Barnum & Bailey circus clown.

Dad began waving at the cars whizzing by, calling out his rendition of "Ho, ho, ho" like an experienced Santa's helper. Though my mother later said that he sounded quite horrible, I'm sure Dad gave no thought to his vocal ability. Being jolly old Saint Nick was the most fun he'd had in years.

Before long cars began to slow, windows rolled down and little arms protruded to wave back in his direction. Then a lone car pulled off the road.

The car was an old frost-green Ford station wagon with rust on the hood. First the back passenger door opened, then the front. Two little girls emerged wearing their Sunday best and started toward Santa. Dad moved to the bottom of the steps, sat down and opened his arms to greet them.

"Ho, ho, ho, ho," he said, noticing that the children had been joined by their smiling parents. "Have you both been good little girls this year?" he asked in a jolly Santa voice.

"Yes sir," said the older child who was now sitting on his knee. Her sister, standing close by, nodded in agreement and grinned, advertising a missing front tooth. She was too shy to look at Santa.

Santa winked at the parents and wiggled his eyebrow at

the child on his knee. "So…what can I bring you for Christmas this year?"

"Don't you want to know my name, Santa?"

"Why sure I do, honey." Dad was a little embarrassed for forgetting to ask such an important question.

"I'm Lorene," she said, brushing a lone auburn curl from over her eyes. "This is my little sister, Louise. She can't talk yet. Mommy's mad because she wet all over her dress in the car."

"She did what?" Santa responded forgetting to disguise his voice.

"You know," Lorene continued and leaned forward, rubbing her shoe against Santa's pant leg. "She peed."

Santa stroked his white beard. "Maybe that should be our little secret, right? So what can I bring you for Christmas this year?"

Lorene didn't hesitate. Not only had she memorized a catalog of goodies for herself, she recited a lengthy list for her little sister. During Lorene's presentation, Santa occasionally glanced at the parents, who, by the looks on their faces, were awe-struck at the requests being submitted by their oldest.

From the corner of his eye, Dad noticed another car pulling to the curb, and realized that with all the traffic out that night, he could be swamped in minutes. He considered speeding up the process to accommodate the next round of kids, but his love of the moment overwhelmed common sense. If the kids wanted to see Santa he would oblige.

Dad placed an arm around Lorene's shoulder. "Say, that's quite an impressive list you have. You sure you deserve all those gifts?"

"No," Lorene said boldly. "I want to give some of them to the family down the street. You forgot to visit them last year."

Dad was favorably impressed. He knew full well that Santa missed a few families each year. What struck him as unusual was that Lorene was not only thinking of herself, she had compiled a lengthy list of goods for her sister and a needy family. Santa gave her a kiss and whispered in her ear that he would do all he could to ensure the delivery of extra presents to her house that year.

When it was Louise's turn, she giggled, flashed a shy look at Santa and at the last minute ran to her mother's arms. She wasn't crying or scared, simply at that age when clinging to her mother often seemed like the best option. Santa knew next year would be different. At least he didn't have to worry about a wet child soaking his knee. That would have been a dandy way to break in his son's new Santa suit.

As the children's mother took them back to the car, their father stepped forward. "Good job young fella," he said. "I thought for a second you were the real Santa."

"I am," Dad bellowed, "and thanks for the complement. I'm sixty-six." The man returned to his car and the family sped off with two sets of arms waving good-bye through the open windows.

That wasn't the end of the commotion. Several additional cars slowed, their juvenile occupants waving and hollering, "Santa, Santa." When another car parked and a sizeable group of children tumbled out and headed his way, Dad began to worry about what he had started. It was difficult for vehicles to park completely off the road and he was concerned about everyone's safety. After this family left, he figured he'd better quit for the evening. As if signaled telepathically, my mother began to turn off the outside lights.

Something all of Santa's helpers learn over the years is that nary a child will admit to being bad at any time during the year. By their own estimation, all are little angels.

One child from the second carload broke that rule, and Dad told me about it later. The boy, who was about seven, requested a new bike, a computer game and a ball glove— nothing out of the ordinary. Suddenly he frowned and recalled, "No, wait a minute. I can't have a bike because I hit my sister last week. I can have the computer game and ball glove because I didn't hurt her that much. Yeah... keep the bike this year."

"Kids *do* say the darndest things," Dad marveled. Most Santa helpers I know would agree.

Across the street and down a few houses lived Virgil and Clara Keith, a couple Mother knew from childhood. Clara was wheelchair bound due to arthritis, and Virgil's mobility was also limited. Dad knew that his friends could use some Christmas cheer so he headed across the street still dressed in my Santa costume. Starting up the front walkway he caught himself whistling, and stopped. Everyone on the block knew his habit of whistling and he didn't want to advertise his presence. Three raps on the door and Patsy Keith, the couple's oldest daughter, answered with a bewildered look. Dad divulged his identity in a whisper.

Other families on the street heard the laughter coming from the Keith household that night. Dad gave a very special gift to those elderly folks, a visit from someone who cared. When he finally removed his beard, he realized that he had pulled off a great charade. The Keiths were amazed to learn that the man in the Santa suit was their neighbor, Bob.

Dad never wore a Santa suit again, but he was proud of his one and only night as Santa and talked of it often. Dad was the first person my siblings and I called Santa, and he didn't need a red suit to earn that title. He was generous to others throughout his life, never asking for a thing in return. Since his passing I sometimes find myself stopping to gawk at other helpers in ill-fitting costumes, especially when I hear a terrible rendition of "Ho, ho, ho." I wonder if my dear father is back in the suit playing Santa once again and having a good old time.

Chapter Fifteen

Baby Kaye and the Broken Leg

Less is more, Ernest Hemingway was known to say. Try to write as true a sentence as possible and keep the paragraphs short. I agree in some instances, but not when writing about a doll named Baby Kaye. Even Mr. Hemingway would have found brevity difficult when writing about this walking, talking ball of energy. Broken leg or not, she traveled faster on crutches than most people do on two good legs.

The place was Ogden, Utah, and I was taking a break from my helper routine under a walnut tree behind a hastily built Santa's house on the edge of an outdoor mall.

For two hours straight I'd worked without a break, kids hollering and wiggling and, in the case of a few young ones, overflowing their diapers on Santa's knee. In winter a wet lap means a cold lap. I was relieved to see my replacement arrive in the back of a Chevy van.

A sudden explosion startled me. Fireworks burst overhead and streaks of multicolored streamers fell to earth. It was unusual to see a fireworks display at Christmas, but a new store was celebrating its grand opening and this was the attention grabber. All I cared about was having the remainder of the night off.

After talking to a hundred children, I was beat. I was also locked out of my truck, which contained the change of clothes I badly needed. In addition, the truck was almost out of gas, my billfold was at the North Pole, and I had a bellyache from eating too much junk food. What else could go wrong?

Sprinkles fell from dark clouds overhead. Just another problem to deal with, I figured. The forecast said no rain. Yeah right—even the air smelled wet.

I closed my eyes for a few seconds hoping for a little rest while contemplating a solution to my woes.

"Hello Santa," a young voice squeaked. "Why are you sitting under a tree?"

I opened my eyes as a walnut bounced off my shoulder. A little girl on crutches was staring at me curiously. She wore loose-fitting faded jeans, a zippered jacket and, though no more than six, dark red lipstick. A rip in her pant leg exposed a cast.

"Who are you?" I asked kindly.

"My real name is Kaye but everyone calls me Baby Kaye. How come you're sitting under this tree, Santa?"

"I uh... I was just taking a break from talking to all the children."

"I saw another Santa at your house," she said, pointing. "How can you be here and over there too?"

"He's one of my helpers. I'm getting quite old you know."

"Does he have the same magic power as you have, Santa?"

"Some," I said. "I give all my helpers a little of my power. Not all of it though."

She leaned on a single crutch, holding the injured leg several inches off the ground. A light wind whipped her auburn hair in a frenzy and she tamed it with a brush from her back pocket. "Do you ride a bike, Santa? Or do you ride your sleigh everywhere?"

I looked at her cast. "I mostly use the sleigh. Sometimes I ride a bike. Is that how you broke your leg?"

"Yeah, kind of," she frowned. "I got hit by a car. A policeman ran over me."

"A policeman did that? Why that's hard to believe." I leaned forward and lightly touched a toe that was sticking out of the cast. "It must have been awful being run over by the police."

"Yeah, I guess so," she answered. Then, for no apparent reason Baby Kaye emitted a feline yowl.

"That sounds like a cat crying," I said, getting to my feet and straightening my suit. "Do you like cats?"

"Mr. Higgins, my kitty cat, went to heaven awhile ago. Him and me always talked kitty talk."

She scratched at her leg through the cast, and I noticed that she had no pinkie finger on her right hand. Genetics, I assumed, for her hand looked completely normal otherwise.

"I can't say I've ever heard kitty talk before." I pointed to her cast. "Kind of itchy is it?"

"It's horrible," she came back. "Just horrible, Santa. If you want to get me something nice for Christmas, all I want is for this itch to go away. Can you do magic like that?"

A small twig under the tree caught my eye. "I've got an idea little one." I grabbed the twig. "Let's see if old Santa can remedy this problem. Where's the break, darling?" She pointed low on her leg, close to her foot. The itch was nowhere near the break. I handed her the twig and, guiding her hand with mine, slid the twig a few inches down inside the top of the cast.

"Oh, that's it right there," she sighed.

She wiggled the twig slightly and a smile crossed her face. No toy in the world would have given her half the pleasure she derived from that little twig. She was one of my most satisfied customers that season. She wiggled the twig again and giggled with such delight that I had to laugh. "How's that, Baby Kaye? Did we get rid of that itch yet?"

She stood on both legs, supporting herself with the crutches. "It's gone Santa. No more itch."

I leaned back against the tree. "Now tell me about Mr. Higgins. You said he passed away."

"You know all about him, don't you Santa? I sent a letter telling you what I want for Christmas."

I processed her question and made a common sense call. "I got your letter, Kaye. Let me see now..." I rubbed the tip-end of my beard. "You want a new Mr. Higgins if I remember correctly."

"You do remember," she cried excitedly.

"I always do, little one. I always remember."

Baby Kaye gave me a big hug and patted my belly. The crutches never got in her way. She used them as extensions of her legs. She even balanced on them for several moments, showing me her gymnastic abilities, though I warned her that falling could result in another broken leg. She swung back and forth so high at times that I thought she would do a flip. And she giggled that special giggle that always made me laugh.

"I need to find my mother," Kaye informed me. "I told her I wouldn't go too far." She looked at the dwindling crowd near the Santa house. "I think my sister went to see you... your helper I mean. I'm not going to tell her I met the real Santa," she confided.

She touched the back of my hand before leaving, rubbing it as if to make sure I was real. "You don't have to bring me a new kitty," she said. "Fixing my itch was good enough— unless you really want to." Then with a wide grin and a final giggle she skipped off on her crutches, her bad leg never touching the ground.

Back to my dilemma.

I sat down, leaned against the tree and pondered whether to thumb my way home or spend the evening waiting for Mrs. Claus to come and get me. The back end of my truck was long enough for napping, but how would I explain my presence to passersby, especially if they were children?

A siren and flashing red and yellow lights from a black and white sheriff's car gave me a ray of hope. Surely the police would have mercy and offer me a ride, a free phone call and maybe a few bucks for gas. Embarrassing, but necessary if I wanted to get home.

"Got a problem, Santa?" a deputy called from the passenger window.

"Problem? I've got a major catastrophe, fellas."

"Kind of thought so," the driver responded. "Is there anything we can do?"

"You bet, Sergeant" I said. "My wallet's at home, I've got no cash and I'm almost out of gas. And wouldn't you know, my keys are locked in the truck."

Both men laughed and exited the car. "I believe we have just what you need, Santa," said the officer, waving a Slim-Jim in the air. "I'll have your truck open in a jiffy. You're going to owe me though."

"Don't forget, you're talking to old Kris Kringle gentlemen. I do miracles almost every day."

"Good, good," the other deputy said slyly. "We'll help you out, then you'll help us, right?"

I sensed there was some side dealing going on that I was not yet privy to. The door lock snapped open. "Doesn't take long at all with that gadget. Do you use it often?"

"Quite often, Santa. Say, now that your problem is solved, how about doing us a favor. It won't take more than a half hour of your time. You game, old fellow?"

"You've got a deal gentlemen. But first I'll need to borrow five dollars from one of you so I can make it home. Gas money you know. What's on your mind? Let me guess, you need a Santa's helper tonight."

"Right," they said in unison. "We've got a helper, least wise we did till this morning. The old boy up and disappeared, a real wino. Who knows where he's at. There's a shelter near here for women who've been victims of abuse. Eight little kids in that shelter are flat out dying to see you."

I took off my beard, wig and hat. "Tell you what officers, you lead the way and I'll follow. I'll gas-up when I'm finished."

"Great," the sergeant agreed. He handed me the five dollars for gas.

Both men started for their police car. "Say, Sergeant," the deputy inquired. "What about Baby Kaye? Is she still out here somewhere?"

"She's with her mother and sis, I believe. I'd better make sure." He raised his hand-held radio.

"Baby Kaye?" I interrupted. "You mean the little girl with the crutches?"

He stopped and looked at me questioningly. "Yes. Have you seen her this evening?"

"Matter of fact, she just left. About six with a catchy giggle, right?"

"That's my Baby Kaye," the sergeant answered.

I walked to the car and he opened the door. "She said something about being run over by a policeman. That wouldn't have anything to do with you would it?"

The sergeant's face flushed beet red with embarrassment. "Yeah. Man I feel rotten about it too." His head dropped slightly. "I told her a dozen times to watch out when she was on that bike of hers. She scared me half to death. Then a couple of weeks ago I had lunch at home and when I was backing out of the driveway she rode up behind me. I never saw her."

"You were lucky," I commented. "It could have been much worse."

He sighed. "You've got that right, Santa. Like I said, it breaks me up to think about it. I don't know what I would have done if I'd hurt her worse."

I patted his shoulder. "She's fine, that's what counts. Now, if you don't mind I'm quite beat so lets get this gig over with. Before I forget, thanks for the help and I'll get the money back to you first thing in the morning."

"No hurry, Santa. Take your time," he grinned. "I know where you live."

The evening finished without a hitch. The children at the center were great kids and I suspect many of them had no idea why they were staying there. As usual, what mattered most was the special visit from Santa—and they loved their candy canes.

To this day I remember Baby Kaye's giggle, and all the energy she displayed even though temporarily handicapped by a broken leg. The missing pinkie finger was no disadvantage to her either. If anything, she was more dexterous than most people with a full hand.

There's a sequel to this saga that will have you scratching your head in awe. *Read the next chapter for the rest of the story.*

This crowd of children is about to escort Santa to his place of honor, where the gift-giving and list recitations will ensue.

Chapter 16

A Small World

An individual who dons the red suit at Christmas for the sake of our children must have the patience of the biblical Job. I say this not to bring credit upon myself but to convey my deepest respect and admiration for any Santa's helper who gives time, energy and love to children at Christmas.

More helpers are needed each year to meet the demands of our growing population, yet the numbers are declining. Consequently, those of us who do this job are in greater demand each year.

Lancaster, California. It was one of the busiest years I ever had. There were far too many Santas needed and not enough to go around. Even the malls were crying for help—advertising in newspapers and on bulletin boards. There were signs everywhere asking for helpers. I contemplated taking leave from my day job to lend a hand at hospitals, churches and other places where I considered Santa's involvement necessary.

One afternoon I was talking with a friend who operates

a part-time photography business. He needed a Santa's helper that very evening for a photo shoot with a young couple and their new baby boy. I've had a million photos taken with children, but none by a professional photographer, so this was a perfect opportunity. I could send a set to my children and grandchildren in Texas.

For working under the hot lights I was to be paid twenty dollars an hour, however I pledged my paycheck ahead of time to the Salvation Army, my favorite charity. I was happy to participate in the session and a set of photos was payment enough.

I arrived early at the studio, my outfit packed neatly in a suitcase along with my goodie bag, which hid a few candy canes. Ron, the photographer, met me at the door with a handshake, and I noticed that his fingers looked rather like pork sausages. He was a squatty fellow who doubled over when he walked.

"Whadda-ya-say, Santa," Ron greeted me, his eyes fixing on my suitcase. "I see you're ready to model."

"Ready as I'll ever be, Ron." I quickly scanned the exterior of his shop. The building appeared to be old and in poor repair. "I hope you're not paying an arm and a leg in rent, my friend. If so I've got some land in Australia I'll make you a deal on."

He laughed. "No, matter of fact the rent's rather reasonable. The place looks better inside. Come on in. I'll show you around."

We entered. Inside the walls were white. Except for a few nail holes that had been painted over, apparently without filler, the surface was clean and unblemished. Heavy use had worn traffic patterns in the dull gold carpet that covered the floor in all three rooms. The only furniture was in Ron's studio where a few cameras sat on tripods and an antique pull-down movie screen stood against one wall. A couch and two arm chairs were positioned directly to the front of the screen, and spotlights hung from an adjustable bar barely within reach.

"Not a bad place at all, Ron. I assume there's a bathroom somewhere?" I pointed to the suitcase.

"Down the hallway to the left," he replied, doing a quick time check. "They'll be here any minute. You want to get ready now or wait till they're here?"

"I'll wait a few minutes," I said. "The suit is hot. I'll barbecue under these lights." I examined one of the cameras. "I'll bet this one had a nice price tag."

"Thirty-five hundred without the lenses," Ron answered. He pointed to another camera in the corner. "That one over there set me back even further."

"I'll stick to the throw-aways," I responded. "Shoot the picture, turn the whole thing in and get photographs almost as nice as the big-timers take." We both laughed, but I could tell Ron disagreed.

"Who are these people anyway? A little odd for someone to want a professional photo shoot with Santa isn't it?"

"Not at all. I get a lot of families each year that request pictures with Santa. Most have them done-up for Christmas cards; they send them to all their relatives."

"Is that what these people are planning?"

"Not to my knowledge," he said. "I understand they had a hard time bringing their son into the world and they're celebrating his birth by having a family photo taken for Christmas—with Santa included for the kid's sake. Boy's only two months old so I doubt he'll cause you any trouble."

I grinned. "I've had younger ones than that yank my beard."

The front door squeaked, announcing the arrival of Ron's clients.

"Sounds like we have company," Ron said, starting for the front foyer. "Do you want to meet these people now?"

"I'll meet them in a few minutes. You get acquainted while I get dressed. Be about fifteen minutes or so."

"Fine, I'll get things set up so we can start when you

return. I'll try to keep you away from the lights as much as possible." He disappeared behind a doorway to meet his clients.

Suitcase in hand, I made my way to the bathroom. There would be no need for a grand entrance, a bunch of ho, ho, ho's, or my usual small talk. This was a different sort of engagement. Since the child was still a baby, he wouldn't remember this day. The object was to capture an image on photo paper, after which I'd be just another Santa in a family picture.

I closed the bathroom door, silently thanked Ron for the full length mirror, unzipped the suitcase and proceeded to get ready as I had a thousand times before.

"It's showtime," I said, making a final visual check of my outfit. The beard was a little crooked so I straightened it. The rest of the trimmings appeared to be in place and secure.

I wondered if Ron was expecting me in full garb. He never mentioned whether the photos would be portraits or full length, but I was ready for either. I opened the door, took a deep breath and exited the bathroom prepared for a grueling hour under the lights.

I strolled down the unlit hallway. No hurry now; the ball was in my corner. They could not start without me. I don't know what came over me but a few feet from the studio, I bellowed, "Ho, ho, ho. Is anyone here waiting for old Saint Nick?"

I entered the studio to laughter and mild applause.

Ron's laugh trailed off. "Mr. Santa, I'd like you to meet Mr. and Mrs. Antone... and little Franklin," he added with emphasis.

My eyes went immediately to the wide-eyed, grinning baby. "Hello, Franklin. You're a real cutie-pie aren't you." I grabbed the infant's big toe and was rewarded with a coo.

"Hello Santa," the Air Force major smiled. His uniform was immaculate, his grin like his son's. "I'm Lucus Antone. I appreciate your time this evening." His hand shot out in friendship.

He must have thought he was gripping the control stick of a fighter jet in combat. Tall and well built, with short hair graying at the temples, the major wore his specially tailored uniform proudly, yet impressed me with his down-to-earth demeanor. He would have made an excellent model for an enlistment poster.

"Santa," his spouse said, her voice a soft caress. "I'm Elaine. It's a pleasure meeting you." She extended her left hand graciously.

"I understand that Franklin is two months old," I said. His sky-blue eyes mesmerized me.

Elaine wiped slobber from the baby's chin. "Two months old today."

"Quite a big baby isn't he?"

"Oh, you're so right, Santa," she answered with a frown. "He weighed nine-and-a-half pounds at birth." She rolled her eyes at the major in disgust, as if he alone was responsible for the baby's size.

"Wow, must have been quite an experience." I gave the major a quick once-over and he flashed a sheepish grin. Anyone could see he was quite proud of his big boy.

"Now that we're all acquainted, shall we begin," Ron said, glancing at his wristwatch.

"I'm game," I responded, flapping my coat to reduce the heat that was building under my garment.

Ron had the family take seats on the couch and told me to crouch directly behind them. Then he changed his mind and moved me to the middle of the couch where I held the baby, with a parent on either side. Ron moved to his camera, peeked through the lens and again changed our positions.

"Can't seem to get the right pose," he said, slightly agitated. "Hmm, lets try this." This time he placed the major behind the couch while I held the baby with Elaine at my side.

"No, no that's not going to work either," Ron fussed.

"You're right, Ron." I handed the baby to his mother. "This isn't a good arrangement. It makes me look as if I'm the baby's father." Glancing over my shoulder, I could see that the major agreed.

Ron shook his head. "Yes, I see your point. Let's go back to the original setup. Santa, you take the major's place. Lucus, you go back to the couch. Elaine, you keep holding the baby."

Musical chairs would have been more exciting. All this moving around was raising my body temperature to the boiling point. I held on, did as requested and took my place behind the couch again.

"Yes," Ron's voice rose with excitement. "That's it, that's it. Just what the doctor ordered." He did a little tweaking—the angle of Elaine's arms, the tilt of the baby's head—till every detail pleased his aesthetically trained eye.

"We've got it people. This is going to be a masterpiece." Ron jogged to his camera. "Now smile everyone—you too, Santa."

"What do you mean, smile? No one's going to see my teeth in this shot."

A few giggles from the couch.

"Wait a minute," Elaine interrupted. "The baby is dribbling again." She grabbed a cloth from the diaper bag on the floor and wiped his chin.

"OK, is everybody ready? Here we go... one...two.... Mrs. Antone, Franklin seems to be slouching. Can you hold him up a bit?"

A few more seconds passed and Ron started again. "Let's do it this time folks. And, here we go... one... two...."

Ron's count was disrupted by a series of loud pops and

wheezes, like a flat tire flapping against the pavement. I knew immediately what it was. Baby Franklin had broken wind.

I figured wrong. The aroma of a freshly filled diaper enveloped the room like gas leaking from a stove. Potent is not the correct word. Lethal is a more suitable adjective. Franklin seemed pleased at his accomplishment.

Mrs. Antone scrambled to her feet with the baby and headed for the bathroom, the diaper bag slung over her shoulder. The smell lingered.

The heat inside my suit was becoming intolerable. Off came the jacket, followed by the hat, beard and wig. After a breath of fresh air and a cold Coke, I felt human again and flopped on the couch for a brief rest. Perspiration dripped in my eyes and I wiped it away with a handkerchief.

I shut my eyes for a couple of minutes. So the baby held up the ballgame a few minutes, big deal. What was an hour of my time anyway? My reverie was broken by a sucking sound. I opened one eye and peered to the side as Elaine sat down with the baby, who was making a feast of his thumb. He was happy now, cleaned up and wearing a new Saint Louis Cardinals baseball outfit.

"Let's get this show going again," Ron prodded. He stood behind his camera giving directions. I took my place behind the couch, centered between Elaine and her husband.

"Major, move slightly to the left. Mrs. Antone, hold the baby up a little." Ron raised an eyebrow and gave me a disparaging look. "Santa," he said, "I think you would look better with your outfit on. The beard, the hat?" He pointed to my jacket lying across the back of the couch.

I grabbed my jacket, stuck an arm in the wrong sleeve and tried in vain to shove the other arm in the opposite sleeve. I must have looked like a clown. First the major broke into laughter, then Elaine did likewise.

I stopped dead still, forgetting to breathe for several seconds. I knew that laugh, that giggle. It rang in my ears like a half forgotten song, like music from long, long ago. It couldn't be. The memory that took shape in my mind was over twenty years old. It had happened eight hundred miles from here. What were the odds?

"I'm sorry for laughing," Mrs. Antone apologized. "I've had a tough day and I needed that."

My eyes traveled to her hands. The left was fine, but the right... There it was, four fingers minus the pinkie. Slowly I dropped my arm.

"Excuse me for staring, Mrs. Antone," I sighed. "Your name is Elaine?"

"Yes, yes it is. Is there something wrong?"

"No problem, Ma'am. It's just that... I used to live in Utah. About twenty years ago, I met a little girl with a broken leg. It itched and I showed her how to scratch it through the cast." I paused. "That little girl was named Baby Kaye, and her right pinkie finger was missing."

Elaine handed the baby to the major. She stared at me. "It's you isn't it? It's really you. My family call me Baby Kaye. Elaine is my middle name." A few seconds elapsed in silence as the two of us stared into each other's eyes. Then we embraced like father and daughter. I was at a complete loss for words realizing that the little girl I met way back then was in my arms giving me a hug as she had done so many years before.

"Am I missing something?" Major Antone intervened.

"You won't believe it honey," Elaine replied, backing away. Tears rolled down her cheeks. "I met this man over twenty years ago when I was a little girl. You remember me telling you about the Santa under a tree? Well here he is," she smiled. "He's the Santa I remember from childhood." Again, we hugged.

"I hate to break up this loving moment." Ron sounded annoyed. "Shall we get these pictures done and then all of you can reminisce over old times. My wife is meeting me in an hour for dinner, so if you don't mind..."

"No problem, Ron," I replied. Elaine, Franklin, and the major took their places together on the couch and I knelt behind them just as before, only this time my hand rested on the shoulder of a beautiful young woman—Baby Kaye. I was jubilant.

All of us, including Ron and his wife, had dinner together at Denny's Restaurant. I learned that Baby Kaye had grown up in Utah, finished college, and become a gifted teacher for mentally challenged children. While living near Hill Air Force Base, she met and married Lucus Antone, and they were soon transferred to Edwards Air Force Base in Southern California.

Was our reunion a fete of destiny or just a chance encounter? I don't have an answer. Either way I'm glad it happened.

With the world as small as it is, I could very well meet baby Franklin twenty years from now and play Santa's helper to his first child—if the good Lord agrees with my timing, that is.

A very Merry Christmas to all—and to all, a good life.

For those of you who crave a little more information
about the man in the red velvet suit,
here's the quick tour...

I was born in the rural state of Illinois. A decade later, my family moved to the small town of Winchester, Kentucky, where I discovered my destiny at the tender age of eleven. Inspired by "The Gene Krupa Story" at a local movie theater, I decided to become a world class drummer. Practice was all it would take. After countless hours of beating my mother's pots and pans to oblivion, Mom and Dad gave me a set of Ludwig drums.

Two years later, I started my first band, "The Illusions." My friends and I (Bret Sewell, Jimmy Potts, Donnie Reed and a base player whose name I can't remember) inflicted noisy torture on the entire block. But practice paid off, and the band played quite a few local events.

When I was fifteen, the family relocated to Lexington, twenty miles away. The band hired a new drummer and continued to perform throughout Kentucky for some twenty years after my departure. Time marches on.

Lexington was a big town with lots of opportunities for an up-and-coming drummer. Before long I was playing with a local group. I'll brag a little—I was extremely good for a teenager. As for school, bah-humbug. My parents would drop my brother and me at school on their way to work. Before their car was off school property I was out the back door and heading home to beat and bang on those beautiful Ludwig drums. Mom and Dad didn't have a clue until I was much older.

Did I mention that during my free wheeling teenage years I drag raced a 1969 Plymouth GTX? Well I did. Ha! And the kids today think they invented the sport. Those were good times, but they didn't last long.

With nowhere to go and the draft looming, I joined the Army in 1969. I even signed on for an extra year so that I could avoid Vietnam. Yeah, right! Another recruiter promise that evaporated the minute they had my signature on the dotted line. It took the Army just eleven months to put me through boot camp, advanced training, and then ship my stupid bones to Vietnam.

At this point in my story let me stress that I never attempted to avoid my responsibility to God, family, or the United States Army. For one thing, my father would have killed me. He was a WWII vet who believed every man should serve his country. My brother Ron made us proud by joining the Marines. At the time, my sister Connie was twirling a baton with the high school band. She later became Miss Majorette of Kentucky.

There were some good moments in Vietnam. Bullets didn't fly twenty-four hours a day. I served in the rear echelon and wasn't part of the heavy fighting anyway, though mortar rounds, rockets and lead did fly overhead. Thankfully the enemy wasn't deadly accurate.

On one occasion in Cam Rahn Bay a rocket streaked overhead and the darn thing hit our latrine. What a mess that was. The entire company was hobbled for three days. Come to think of it, maybe the enemy was more accurate then I figured! Shortly thereafter, my convoy found out how accurate the enemy could be when the jeep I was driving was hit by fire, lodging shrapnel in my knee and ankle.

A war that should not have been fought? Yes, I agree, but I did my duty along with hundreds of thousands of other GIs. And except for the added weight of metal in my bones, everything Vietnam gave to me was good. I played my first Santa gig there, and knew in my heart that my drumming days were over.

Back in the states and out of the service, I moved around a bit trying to support a growing family. I sold cars, worked in a 7-Eleven, did odd jobs and went back to school to finish my education. Then I took the advice of my parents and hired on with the U.S. government, working first at Hill Air Force Base in Ogden Utah, and finishing my career at Edwards Air Force Base in Southern California.

Sometimes things we do in our youth return to haunt us. A few years ago I took my wife Annie to a drag race and found out that she had always wanted to drive fast cars. These days, we race almost every weekend. She's an exceptional driver and has the trophies to prove it. (What a woman!)

Today when I change into that red velvet suit, everything's just like it was 30 years ago. The thrill is still there, though I move a little more slowly these days. My only regret is that I never played Santa for my own three wonderful children. The deception never would have worked—they knew their father's voice too well—still, not a Christmas goes by that I don't wish I could revisit those days and give it a try.

I no longer play drums, but one of my hobbies is rebuilding old worn out sets for kids who can't afford to buy new. I recently refurbished a set for my grandson (to date I have seven terrific grandchildren). He was astonished to receive a family heirloom along with the set. I restored my old Ludwig snare drum and conferred it on the boy with six hours of instruction.

"Thanks, Dad," was my daughter's response. "Thanks a lot!"

I could hear drumming in the background.

Robert Clifton (RC) Goodman Jr.
SirRCGoodman@aol.com

Titles Published by Aslan

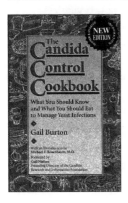

The Candida Control
Cookbook What You
Should Know And What
You Should Eat To
Manage Yeast Infections
by Gail Burton
$14.95
ISBN 0-944031-67-6

Workout for the Soul: 8 Steps
to Inner Fitness
by Chrissie Blaze
$14.95
ISBN 0-944031-90-0

The Gift of Wounding:
Finding Hope & Heart
in Challenging
Circumstances
by Andre Auw Ph.D.
$13.95
ISBN 0-944031-79-X

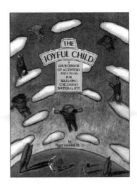

Solstice Evergreen: The
History, Folklore & Origins of
the Christmas Tree
2nd ed by Sheryl Karas
$14.95
ISBN 0-944031-75-7

Intuition Workout: A
Practical Guide To
Discovering & Developing
Your Inner Knowing
by Nancy Rosanoff
$12.95
ISBN 0-944031-14-5

The Joyful Child:
A Sourcebook of Activities
and Ideas for Releasing
Children's Natural Joy
by Peggy Jenkins Ph.D.
$16.95
ISBN 0-944031-66-8

Sing and Change the World
By David Edward Dayton, $16.95; ISBN 0-944031-92-7

The Sacred Weave
By Marianne Franzese Chasen, $13.95; ISBN 0-944031-91-9

To order any of Aslan's titles send a check or money order for the price of the book plus Shipping & Handling

　　　Book Rate $3 for 1st book.; $1.00 for each additional book
　　　First Class $4 for 1st book; $1.50 for each additional book

Send to: ***Aslan Publishing**
　　　2490 Black Rock Turnpike # 342
　　　Fairfield CT 06825

To receive a current catalog: please call (800) 786–5427 or (203) 372–0300
E-mail us at: **info@aslanpublishing.com**
Visit our website at **www.aslanpublishing.com**

Our authors are available for seminars, workshops, and lectures. For further information or to reach a specific author, please call or email Aslan Publishing.